HAVING PEOPLE OVER

HAVING PEOPLE OVER

*A Modern Guide to Planning, Throwing,
and Attending Every Type of Party*

Chelsea Fagan

PHOTOGRAPHS BY CHELSEA KYLE
ILLUSTRATIONS BY LAYLA FULLER

TEN SPEED PRESS
California | New York

*This book is dedicated to the women
of my family, who make the everyday
feel impossibly glamorous.*

CONTENTS

INTRODUCTION

Letter from Chelsea

DEAR HOSTESS,

For as long as I can remember, my family's house was the party house. More weekends than not, people gathered at our home for all kinds of celebrations: dinner parties, theme parties, poker parties, and countless other mini-events. As the guests began to arrive, my parents would implore my sister and me to greet them, maybe share a charming anecdote from school, before banishing us to their bedroom, where we'd enjoy the snacks and movie rental with which they'd bribed us. As long as we didn't disturb anyone, we could stay up as late as we wanted, bouncing on the bed while the din of laughter wafted up toward us, eventually lulling us to sleep.

I remember the ritual of it: the days spent preparing dishes and decorations and the near-endless cleaning, even of spaces guests would never see. In some ways, our lives revolved around this constant expanding and contracting of our home, the buzzing promise of visitors turning our space into a kind of living entity. And life never felt more complete than when the house was full of lively music and the sound of people filling their plates.

My mother was always head chef and chair of the decorations committee in our home, with the rest of us following her vision (these days, my mother favors a subdued interior palette of creams, dark browns, and brass finishes). And to this day, my father is happy to play executive assistant. When you're a guest in their home, he is still her biggest hype man, drawing your attention to something she did particularly well. *"Isn't that dip amazing?"* he'll say, handing you a drink perched on a cocktail napkin. *"It was so hard not to eat the whole thing before you arrived."* Especially in the early days of my childhood, when money was very tight, my mother's unique talent for making something of nothing wasn't just what lit up their parties: It was what kept our lives from feeling as difficult as they actually were. We were often rolling quarters to pay the bills, but homemade food for parties and handmade costumes on Halloween made the limitations feel like creative exercises.

Although the spaces I've lived in through my own adult life share little with the homes I grew up in, I'm proud to say that I've kept the tradition of entertaining at the center of my solar system. In a given week, my husband Marc and I will host at least one gathering, and

we've selected a group of friends who love to entertain as much as we do.

Don't get me wrong: I relish a good restaurant or a night out dancing, the see-and-be-seen exhilaration of being in a crowd. But there is something so beautiful about welcoming people into your home, taking time to prepare an experience for them, and sharing the intimate, beautiful tedium of your life. Whether a raucous cocktail party that spans social groups or a cheeky grown-up slumber party with one of my favorite women, hosting is the center of my life.

Of course, even if there were no greater significance to the act of hosting, I would still love doing it: Having people over is incredibly fun. But I would argue that, in a culture that is increasingly estranged from itself, with communities fraying at the edges, gathering is an important act. We can get into the sociopolitical details later, but suffice it to say that bringing people together is one of the most powerful things we can do right now. We were meant to be a village, and that village was meant to gather in the home.

Rarely is this clearer to me than when I consider my relationship to those in my life with children. I decided long ago that parenthood was not for me—a choice that often results in people warning me of the dire lack of community I'll experience as I age. But so far, I've found the opposite is true: I have plentiful energy to connect with the mothers in my life and delight in the opportunity to have kids around. Bringing new moms food and gift baskets, hosting them for casual gatherings where they're welcome to bring the whole family, creating events where mothers and non-mothers alike can mingle at their own pace: I love being a part of the experience in my own small way, being intentional about the community I create. Cultivating a space that opens its doors to people in all stages of life is one of the most essential human activities.

I also believe hosting is uniquely adaptable to all different budgets, in a way that few things today are. Looking back, a big part of the reason my parents defaulted to hosting at home was because of its affordability. And as someone who has staked most of her career on financial transparency and education, and on the realities of going from low income to a much more comfortable tax bracket, I can honestly say that entertaining is something I've been able to do at every income level. I hosted potlucks and movie nights when I was at my most broke—sometimes relying on them to stock me with leftovers for the week to come—and now I throw lavish gatherings for friends and family, because nothing is more worthy of disposable income than sharing it with others.

While I cannot promise that every single idea or tip in this book will be relevant to everyone, I *can* promise that the vast majority can be implemented across the financial spectrum. Being a good host is about making people feel welcome, about creating moments that feel special and intentional—and so much of that has nothing to do with money. The entire point of reframing your social life in this way is to unlearn the idea that you need extravagant (and expensive) nights out to solidify a friendship or feel like you're getting the most out of life.

Similarly, I want to posit the (perhaps radical) idea that becoming a hostess is about deciding that your platonic relationships are just as important as your romantic or familial ones. I *love* my friends—meaningfully, enthusiastically, joyously—and welcoming them into my home is an important way to demonstrate and reinforce that. Much of what we will talk about in this book is the art of maintaining and strengthening relationships even as our lives change, when we don't have the effortless convenience of school or work to bring us together.

This book will also examine what it means to be a good guest, because showing up as our best selves is just as important as welcoming others into our spaces. What to bring, when to arrive, the thank-yous and follow-ups that make a host feel appreciated—they are all important.

There are few more wonderful things in life than being the kind of person others want to invite over, the person whose presence lights up a party or makes the host's life that much easier. Hosting is about giving in many ways, but it is also about receiving, and learning to be an ideal guest ensures that you're always holding up your end of the bargain.

I think often about what my childhood home was like during party nights, how so many small efforts accumulated to create an experience that seemed totally effortless. There was a warmth on those evenings, an invisible electricity that buzzed and hummed among all the guests and rose all the way upstairs, even as my sister and I were removed from the thick of things. It is that electricity I strive for, the moment just before the party is at its peak, when everyone is engaged in great conversation, feeling unusually attractive and charming, buzzed as much from the magic of the moment as from anything they might have imbibed.

For those who did not grow up learning how to build these moments—how to create a home for entertaining, how to properly stock a kitchen, what recipes to make, how to curate the flow of an evening, et cetera—I understand that it can all seem intimidating. It can also seem overwhelming, because there are so many little things you could overlook or do imperfectly. But I can promise that the smallest effort goes a long way, especially in our culture, which has largely forgotten the art of hosting. Taking the time to arrange a few things on a tray, to set up a beverage station, to ask in advance about dietary needs and actually accommodate them, to curate a playlist for the evening: These small touches are all easy to pull off, and range from "free" to "very inexpensive." And when they are done well and with intention, your guests will be blown away at the seamlessness of the evening.

Being a true hostess isn't complicated or expensive. It is simply the act of treating the people who come into your home with care and celebrating the moments you're lucky enough to share with them.

Everything else is just decoration.

Chelsea

Chapter One

WHAT HAPPENED TO HOSTING?

IN 1922, EMILY POST PUBLISHED her seminal book, *Etiquette*. It was a massive achievement (even in terms of word count, clocking in at over seven hundred pages) and provided guidance for nearly every aspect of then-modern life. More than a hundred years later, she remains a reference point for manners, despite the fact that her name has also become shorthand for outdated, overly stringent social rules. (The Emily Post Institute, formed to continue her legacy, actually provides a surprising level of flexibility on certain issues. For example, they think it's acceptable to wear white to a wedding, provided you do not take attention away from the bride. Shocking!)

Emily Post's career led to a democratizing of social graces that was completely unprecedented. In fact, her entire life was unusual for a woman of her time. She was born into wealth and social prestige, but started her career in earnest as a writer and eventual society expert after her sons were off at boarding school. Even then, she published many works, including several novels, before becoming the Emily Post we're familiar with relatively late in her career. She also divorced her husband for cheating on her, an unusual act at the time. In some ways, her life and career trajectory feel quite modern. Yet in reading her work today, it's almost impossible to imagine any one person having such a monopoly on communicating what is considered polite. If nothing else, the comically matter-of-fact tone she uses throughout *Etiquette* would be considered incredibly tone-deaf by most modern readers.

While she may still be the most prominent voice of etiquette in American society, the concept of detailed social norms dictating our interactions is nothing unique. Every culture and every

historical period had their own quirky expectations around how we should interact, from Victorian England discouraging gentlemen from speaking to women unless they had first been spoken to, to the politically complicated rules around fingernail length in the Chinese Imperial Court, with the Emperor's being the longest.*

How we present ourselves and how we receive others in public has always been fraught, with micro-interactions occurring simultaneously on top of the actual meaning of what we're saying. Eye contact, handshake grip strength, even, apparently—according to some very dreary male podcasters—how straight we stand relative to members of the opposite sex: All of this can be imbued with meaning and can speak for us before we even open our mouths.

Add to these dynamics the fact that America is incredibly diverse culturally speaking, and you have a situation where rather than one dominant idea of what is "right," you have a million competing versions of it. Emily Post's influence lingers in America today in part because it represents a much more monocultural era with clearer class divisions. Although America was still quite diverse during her time, there was a much more limited group of people making the rules about what it meant to be a proper American in polite society. Since her era, and particularly since the explosion of communication the internet has brought, there has not been a singular voice that defined American culture as it pertains to social graces—at least not at her scale. And while this is undoubtedly a positive thing and has resulted in a more pluralistic,

---

* *The Habits of Good Society: A Handbook of Etiquette for Ladies and Gentlemen,* 1859.

culturally nuanced, and (relatively) equal society, it also means less clarity around how we expect to treat one another.

In our contemporary culture, there has definitely been a sharp turn away from the worst excesses of "social graces." And, in many ways, this is a good thing! We have more freedom to wear the clothes we want in the settings we want, approaching someone for courtship is just an app download away, and women don't have to walk around with a chaperone in order to preserve their modesty. But this dissolution of our most limiting social structures has also been a turn toward the aggressively casual—often to the point of indifference. The "cool girl" monologue from *Gone Girl* may have most expertly described it, at least as it pertains to women, but our paradigm is clearly one of "not making a big deal of things." And in a digital world where everyone has access to limitless knowledge, especially about each other, being low-key even to the point of aloofness is considered chic. We don't want to be the first (or last) to text, and we're not overly concerned with showing up on time. If the hoodie was the ultimate symbol of the tech revolution, our overall approach to social interaction has taken on a distinctly "hoodie" energy, as well.

Combine this trend toward the casual with the twin realities of poorly regulated capitalism and toxic self-care culture, and we're in a pretty strange environment. People are working longer hours for lower wages—which largely haven't kept pace with inflation since the late 1970s—and they simply don't have time for social lives. Similarly, our well-intentioned but often insufficient discourse around mental health has been primarily focused on the individual, with "setting boundaries" being one of the most common refrains. And this makes sense, right? Just like our Emily Post–era norms around etiquette were overly strict and oppressive, we used to have social ties that completely violated the wellness of the individual at the cost of the collective—as any eldest daughter might attest throughout history. Women were expected to tolerate everything up to and including abuse in order to maintain a sense of peace in social groups. When you consider how much the average person is being overworked, it's reasonable that the pendulum would swing to a place where the community is a distant second to the self.

So, we may be more insulated, and, through our casualness, less at risk of seeming too eager or vulnerable, but we are also losing a lot. The network of small favors and connections that once flourished in the absence of ultra-convenience has begun to wither away. We can call an Uber rather than have a friend pick us up from the airport. We can just have groceries delivered when we're sick, rather than having a neighbor bring us food. We don't even feel the need to reach out and catch up with people, because we see a constant highlight reel of their lives on social media. On the surface, we might say that this reduces headaches for everyone and makes life easier, but the truth is those tiny little moments of mutual reliance actually make us happier in the long run. (In fact, there's even great data on the fact that *giving* gifts makes us much happier than receiving them—up to the point of having actual, demonstrable health benefits!*)

---

* "How to Make Giving Feel Good," by Elizabeth Dunn and Michael Norton, Great Good Magazine, June 18, 2013, https://greatergood.berkeley.edu/article/item/how_to_make_giving_feel_good.

It's no surprise that in this context, things such as dinner parties were first on the chopping block. Yes, we can see an overall trend that people are hosting less in their homes than they have in previous generations, but we can also see that more foundational things such as the nightly family dinner have declined sharply as well. Gathering, even with the people we already live with, has been cast aside as an inconvenience. And I want to be clear—both about this, and about everything we're going to discuss in this book—that this is not a choice for some. Many people work long hours, well into the evening, and would love to spend more time with their families but simply cannot. Many people would love to host their friends but are geographically isolated or financially unable to spare the expense. There are ways in which our modern lives intentionally separate us from each other and make even the most basic social interactions feel impossible, but this is not true for everyone.

There are many people—we all know them, or maybe we *are* them—who simply feel unable to foster their relationships, even if it's hurting them in the long term. It's simply easier to swipe on their phones through dinner, ignoring the person sitting across from them. They enjoy seeing friends sometimes but are only used to doing so in an overpriced restaurant or bar where everything is taken care of for them. They don't reach out for favors and don't grant them for others because they don't want to be a burden, and there's always an app that can help in a pinch. For what it's worth, I do not blame people for ending up in a place where their relationships are at the very bottom of their priority lists —even those with plenty of resources. Outside of our romantic partners, and maybe

occasionally our family members, we're not really given a good education on how to maintain these connections or even understand
why they are important. Friendships are often treated as a luxury, a
nice-to-have but not a need-to-have.

And then there is the actual *hosting* of it all. Beyond just
meeting up with friends for a dinner out or a concert, the act of
having people over can feel incredibly intimidating. Home decor
and interior design saturate our social feeds more than ever before,
but so much of it is just over-aspirational nonsense that doesn't
relate to our lives. With so much focus on aesthetics and less on
maintenance—and we'll discuss that later in the book—we are
often in spaces that are barely put together enough for *ourselves*
most days, let alone a group of visitors. Besides, that constant look
into homes of those wealthier and more fabulous than us only
makes us feel inadequate in comparison. Our places don't look like
the ones we see on any of our screens, so why should we bother
inviting people into them? Hosting now often feels like a relic of
a time when someone was staying home all day to clean and prep,
and we weren't constantly comparing ourselves to people we don't
even know in real life.

Then there is the art of being *hosted*. If you were to read the
original *Etiquette* today, in addition to many of the rules feeling
laughably specific and arbitrary, you would mostly be overwhelmed
at the idea of living in a society that imposes so many expectations on basic interactions. And I agree that moving away from this
model is largely a good thing: In addition to being incredibly strict,
the entire concept of "manners" has always been intertwined with

racism, sexism . . . essentially every kind of -ism. As I mentioned earlier, Emily Post's success was in part because she was the "right" kind of woman to be giving the advice: old money wealthy, white, a (former) wife, and mother. What is considered "polite" often has as much to do with the person themselves as the actions they are taking.

But the laissez-faire attitude toward social interactions and amorphous social boundaries of today, as well as a lack of agreed-upon standards, can have sharp downsides. One only needs to scroll through social media to see countless videos of people ghosted by their friends, fighting over group trip budgets, or being baffled by the behavior of the potential dates they're meeting via apps. We don't all know what the rules are, and this makes the thought of being a guest incredibly fraught.

If I may be so bold, I'd like to present a third option, a middle ground between the ultra-strict etiquette of the past and the social chaos of today: the art of active communication. We don't need to memorize a labyrinthine series of rules just to have lunch with a friend, but we do need to be up front about our expectations and be ready to listen to theirs. If we're going to be late, we can send a message. If being on time is very important, we can share that ahead of time. Rather than constantly waiting for the other person to read our minds, we can extend to them the grace of certainty about how we feel.

I hear very often when I share my hosting content online that it's "old-fashioned," or, sometimes, "gives auntie vibes." I always take this as a compliment (even if it isn't intended as one), and I agree on some level: It's not nearly as common today to host more formal gatherings, or to make doing so central to one's identity. And I think, in addition to all the reasons we've just discussed, there is a misconception that in order to embrace those old rituals, you also have to embrace the oppressive notion of etiquette that used to accompany them. I don't know the "proper" way to arrange flatware or fold napkins, I don't always serve things in the "right" order, and I am constantly caught with my elbows on the table. But I believe that hosting can be about embracing active communication over "manners" and being imperfect rather than putting on a tiring show for each other.

In order to reclaim these hosting traditions, we will need to lose what was always less desirable about them, and free ourselves from the ever-increasing pressure to make things look a certain way. We don't need to compare ourselves to some pristine influencer's dining room in order to invite people for dinner, nor do we need to put the exact proper language on the "save the date" cards. It doesn't matter if we must frantically Google "what is black tie?" and still get it wrong because we don't have the proper clothing for it. If we can take our distaste for overly formal interactions and combine it with a love for gathering in intimate spaces, we will have the recipe for something truly fabulous on our hands.

"For me, hosting is an expression of love and care, and I believe strongly that it should be done from a place of joy rather than obligation. Everything flows from the delight in the act of hosting, and I work (sometimes very hard) to let go of other expectations in service to what will be most joyful for myself, my husband (so often my co-host), and our guests. I would encourage hosts to explore the 'why' behind a gathering—from something as loaded with 'tradition' and 'expectation' as a wedding or a holiday party, to a more casual dinner or picnic— and to unpack any aspects that feel like they might be out of guilt or obligation. I think it's better to leave those aspects behind—rituals, structures, fancy trappings, even invitations that feel like they are more about what you 'should' do rather than what you want to do as a host can be reconsidered, and in some cases re-invented or omitted from your gathering to let your light really shine and genuinely connect you and your guests."

—ROXANNE EARLEY, URBANIST AND CERAMIC MAKER

Chapter Two

THE BEST THINGS IN LIFE ARE FREE

WHEN YOU GROW UP WITHOUT much money, you never know which financial memories will stick with you. There were ways that this lack of resources felt freeing—we were used to not having a lot, so even the smallest luxuries felt extremely indulgent—but there were also vast limitations. I remember certain homemade outfits that I longed to throw in the trash because all I wanted at the time was the brand-name item the cool girls were wearing. (The immense gift of having a mother who made custom clothing for me was, unfortunately, mostly lost on an eight-year-old.) And even as I got older and money became more stable, I remember certain things as sharply today as I do the most tentpole moments of my life. There are certain brands I still wince to look at because I remember how ruthlessly I was mocked for trying to pass off my cheap knockoff versions. When a certain, very vulnerable chord of financial insecurity was struck, it formed a core memory that I often think will never be fully forgotten.

My childhood scarcity mindset, combined with moving to an affluent area as a preteen, resulted in crippling insecurity around money, which spiraled into credit card debt, debt collectors, and winding up every two weeks at different check-cashing places just to get by. (If you want a much more in-depth explanation on all of this, I recommend my second book, *The Financial Diet.*) My extreme anxiety about money and appearance felt like a monster constantly threatening to consume me and derail every other area of my life in which I'd made progress.

And yet, even when navigating the turbulent and often deceptive friendships of one's early twenties, I still wanted to throw cool parties, to have people over, and to cook up interesting dinners in my meager studio apartment kitchens and have people enjoy them. Even if I didn't have a sliver of the resources I do now, financially or emotionally, I wanted to bring people together and feel their warmth in my home, and I mostly made it work.

One night, though, at a particularly well-lubricated dinner party, a very wealthy friend broke one of my wine glasses. I recall it vividly because I knew even in my late-night haze that this was something I couldn't afford to replace, even though the glass likely only cost a few dollars from IKEA. My budget was incredibly tight, and just getting food together for guests stretched it as thin as it would go, so I remember the radiating anxiety that moved up my spine as I plastered a smile on my face, and he went to grab a water glass to continue drinking wine from. It was nothing to him, and I knew that. In order to maintain that social connection, I had to do my best to pretend that it was nothing to me either. That's how these things work.

Even more distinctly, though, I remember what happened the next day. On his way home from work—yes, in those days we held raucous, up-til-two-a.m. dinner parties on school nights—he rang my buzzer and dropped off, with no ceremony whatsoever, a gorgeous set of six Bordeaux wine glasses. They were from one of the fancier home-goods stores in the area and were of such exquisite beauty and craftsmanship that I nearly broke into tears unpacking them. I remember the generous shape of their curve, their large size, their long, ultra-thin stems, the incredibly satisfying *ting* sound they made when you clinked two of them together.

They were immediately the nicest thing in my apartment, and it felt almost unreal that someone could just purchase a set without a second thought to replace a single broken IKEA glass. *That* is what money looks like, I thought: a total fluidity of experience that allows you to focus on what you want, without ever really worrying about what you need, because all of that is taken care of.

Twelve years later, I still feel that way about money. Being financially secure now, I honestly think about money mostly in terms of *not* having to think about it. If I were to break a glass in someone's home today, I would do the exact same thing as my friend did many years ago. But I remember how miraculous it felt to me at the time, and how it gave me a sliver of hope that while there would always be differences between myself and some of the people in my life, the right sense of community can override that, if only for an evening. Because he had money, sure, but an evening at his house consisted of a few bottles of beer he forgot to put in the refrigerator and an unopened bag of chips on the coffee table. He didn't have a sense of curation or social effort, maybe because he didn't really need to. I could not afford the same things, but when he came to my apartment, he stepped into a different world, where all of these things were taken care of.

Whenever I am hosting, I like to think first and foremost about the ways I can make it feel special that *aren't* about spending more money. This is in part because I learned early on how to do things on an ultra-tight budget, but also because I never want to fall into the common trap of buying more *things* when the real task is putting in more *care*. I don't want to betray that twenty-three-year-old who nearly burst into tears when someone broke a single wine glass; I want to keep the sense of warmth and intimacy that is accessible to everyone, that doesn't leave anyone feeling as if they're not good enough to be part of the group.

For me, this starts with food. While on very rare occasions I will break out things such as caviar, real champagne, and exquisite cuts of meat, I usually prefer not to. I like braising the tougher cuts over long afternoons, getting creative with how I serve a potato, or making miracles out of canned fish or beans. I don't bother with fancy fresh pasta; boxes of the dry stuff are fine. I like making my own salad dressings because it's way better for a fraction of the price. I can name a dozen sparkling wines that are just as good as champagne but don't come with the luxury connotations and are therefore much more affordable. I usually potluck-style outsource

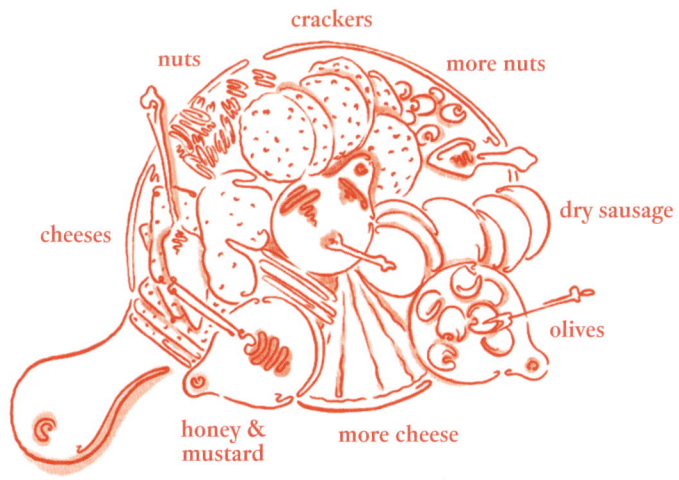

dessert to a friend who loves to bake—as I do not—rather than get some fancy tart from an overpriced bakery. I like food that feels simple and accessible, even at dinner parties.

Similarly, for decor, I try to always opt for frugality. I tie my napkins with a string of twine, I have exactly as many plates and bowls as I need, and I keep a total of two table runners and one tablecloth in the linen closet for special occasions. I love making a centerpiece, but mine are almost always composed of fresh fruit, dried flowers, taper candles, or other items I have in rotation that cost almost nothing and, in some cases, can be eaten with dessert. I'll make place cards with folded pieces of construction paper or fluff up some festive paper cocktail napkins in wine glasses for a functional bit of decoration. There are plenty of ways to make a space feel special and unique that cost almost nothing and, contrary to what social media would have us believe, we do not need to overhaul our style for every new season or holiday.

I, obviously, have more expensive parties now than I did in my twenties (among other things, I have reached the age where if I'm drinking, it's only very high-quality stuff). I can afford to forget things and run out at the last minute, or go a little more overboard for certain special occasions. But I still remember very well the following rules I lived by when I was hosting on a basically-nothing budget, which I use every time I host.

- **TELL YOUR GUESTS WHAT TO BRING.** We will break down the ins and outs of guest etiquette later, but here's the deal: A seasoned host needs to be okay with prompting people on what to bring. Most guests know not to show up empty-handed, but most do not know what is welcome or what could be annoying to receive. I like to send out invites along with a message like "Your presence is more than enough, but if you would like to bring something, X or Y would be much appreciated." People are smart. They'll figure out the rest.

- **CANNED FOOD IS YOUR FRIEND.** Many of my most crucial hosting dishes are made from humble tinned foods. (Side note: I feel like tinned is sort of the sexy word for canned food, and I like that it's having a renaissance!) Either way, these foods are often incredibly inexpensive, versatile, and most importantly last *forever* in your cabinet, so you can always find a use for them down the road. Go, canned food!

- **IT'S ALL ABOUT PRESENTATION.** We've all been to that party where the host has unthinkingly tossed a family-size bag of Tostitos Scoops and an open jar of Pace salsa on the kitchen island in the way of an hors d'oeuvre. And I'm not saying you can't have the Tostitos and salsa. But I *am* saying to get a large bowl and a small one, put the chips in the large bowl and spoon the salsa into the small bowl, and top it with some fresh cilantro or sliced jalapeños. Whatever you're serving, remove it from the packaging, doctor it up even the tiniest bit, and you've instantly upgraded the whole vibe of your party.

- **POTLUCKS ARE ALWAYS AN OPTION.** When I was at my most frugal, basically every party I threw was some kind of a potluck. And you'd be surprised at how many people enjoy them, either because they like to show off their own cooking skills, or because they want to ensure one of their favorite foods will be served. Either way, there is no shame in a potluck, and there are many great themes that naturally lend themselves to the format: '70s rec room, fall harvest, and Spanish tapas are a few of my personal favorites.

- **SET THE MOOD FIRST AND FOREMOST.** Many aspects of mood-setting are free or extremely low-cost: good lighting, a set table, a vibey playlist, lit candles, enough places for everyone to sit. All of these things help the experience feel elevated and intentional, without requiring a host to go into credit card debt to achieve.

- **WHIMSY OVERRIDES IMPERFECTION.** In my opinion, swap in whimsy wherever perfection can't be achieved (which is basically always). Lean into mismatched, thrift-store table settings. Serve foods family-style. Play parlor games that don't require learning a lot of complicated rules. Give yourself permission to just have fun, rather than obsess over everything feeling "grown-up"—or perfect.

I'm not going to be one of those now-affluent people who gets nostalgic for a time when they had less money. That's kind of insulting (*Bitch, if you miss it that much, give your money away*).

But I will say that the rampant lifestyle inflation we see among the wealthy and the social damage and isolation that money can create doesn't have to be the default. Most of us, if we're being thoughtful, can identify things in our lives that bring us great joy while costing little money. We can opt out of a lot of consumer culture (more on that in Chapter 11), and we can make conscious choices to be happy with less.

In some ways, hosting is the perfect opportunity to embrace this mentality, as it is fundamentally not about any one thing you are buying, but rather about the experience you are creating. I wish I could go back and be a guest at one of my parties when I was twenty-two to experience it from the outside. I remember them being so fun, so intimate, and filled with warmth in my teeny little apartment, where we had to pretend my bed wasn't eight feet from the dining table.

I would like to see that Chelsea drink out of her dinky little IKEA glasses and bask in the glow of the taper candles she saved up to afford so everyone would look beautiful across the dinner table. I would tell her that although she doesn't have much right now, and that can make her feel worthless sometimes, she already has the building blocks of everything she'll ever need. She knows who is important, and she takes time to show them how much she loves them. The rest will come in time.

Chapter Three

CREATING A
SEXY SPACE

THERE ARE CERTAIN HOMES YOU walk into and immediately feel captivated by. These homes tell a story, they create a mood, and they feel like an escape from whatever world you left behind when you walked through the door. This has nothing to do with the particular style of decor and everything to do with personality. In fact, I would argue that the most fabulous homes are the ones that feel in some ways out of style, not perfectly in good taste—something you have to experience in person rather than scroll by on a social media feed.

These are homes that truly reflect the people who live in them, are full of their histories and preferences and idiosyncrasies. I love all sorts of them: slinky mid-century modern homes, quirky-yet-simple Nordic homes, chintzy maximalist homes, and everything in between. I mostly want to feel as if I am meeting you when I enter, like I'm getting to spend a few hours inside your brain. And I have found that the more the home feels personal to a host, the easier it is for them to create an experience optimized for guests—which usually means optimized for *sexiness*.

When I'm going for a dinner or cocktail party, I want to feel *sexy*. The space itself doesn't have to feel sexy—no need to throw red lace over the lamp shades!—but the people entering it should. And what makes a space sexy? I think it's simple: There should be great lighting, comfortable places to sit, and food and drink thoughtfully arranged for guests' arrival. There should be music, but not too loud. There should be a flow to the evening, a movement and life to the gathering, secret pockets where hushed conversations are happening (usually, the best ones are in the kitchen). There should be a frisson of possibility, the feeling that anything could happen, and you would be delighted to go along with it. The right space and the right attention to detail will make your guests feel like the best and most charming version of themselves, effortlessly. And although it may sound intimidating, no matter your personal style, the ingredients for making people feel great in your home are quite simple. It's all about paying attention to the sensory experience and anticipating how your guests might feel as they move through the evening.

Creating a sexy space is really a two-step process. There is the space you curate generally, and then there is what you do to it before guests arrive. To make things simpler, I'm going to separate these two and start with the heavier lift: your actual home decor. For the purpose of expedience, we are going to focus exclusively on living spaces. Most of this will apply to other rooms' decor, too, but since gatherings are most likely to occur in your dining and living rooms (often one and the same here in New York), I want to talk about what you're doing there. If you're already a master of interior design who has created your ideal space, feel free to skip ahead—but if you're totally new or stuck somewhere in the process, here is how I think about creating an intentional space.

I am extremely methodical about decor. I believe that whether you're renting or buying, the stakes of making alterations to your home are pretty high. Not only does furniture cost a lot, actually breaking out the tools and building or mounting things is a commitment. (Have you ever installed a heavy and cumbersome shelving unit only to discover you wanted it to be about four inches lower? I have!) So, to this end, I follow a process when planning any home improvements, from the totally decorative, like hanging a great piece of thrift-store artwork, to the five-figure renovation. Here's what I do:

- **GATHER INSPIRATION.** For every day I actually spend implementing my decor plans, I spend at least ten days setting up a mood board. I scour social media, physical magazines, Google search results, coffee table books, and basically every source I can think of to hone ideas and learn what I actually like. I find that diversifying the material (especially in terms of era—I love looking at vintage decor magazines!) helps steer me away from temporary trends toward a more timeless idea of my actual style.

- **SKETCH IT OUT.** I have an actual physical sketchbook I use for planning anything decor-related. Not only do I make a drawing of what I have in mind (I'll often trace photos from my phone to be super-accurate with proportions), I will color things in, add paint swatches, and collage with inspiration pics.

- **INVENTORY.** Whether it's furniture, paintings, housewares, tools, leftover paint, or anything else I might need for a project, I always inventory what I have before I even think of buying something new. If my sketches and mood board lead me to a potential purchase, I have to first establish that I don't already have what I need to (mostly) make it happen.

• **MAKE A PURCHASE PLAN.** As with anything you're about to spend money on, you never want to go in blind, budget-wise. Especially when it comes to home furnishings, costs can easily spiral, so you want to price out everything you need *before* you start shopping.

• **HUNT!** When it comes to home decor, you should rarely pay retail price (and should very rarely need to buy something new). Take advantage of estate sales, flea markets, Facebook Marketplace, and vintage shops: Unless it's something you absolutely, desperately need right now (and that is rare), you are better off being patient and finding a great deal.

• **TAPE EVERYTHING OUT.** People joke that before I do anything decor-wise, my place looks like a basketball court with all the dimensions taped out over the floors and walls. If that's the case, so be it. Measurements and proportions can take you by surprise. Tape things out so you know exactly what you're getting into: That means furniture, art placement, television mounting, and everything in between.

• **DO IT!** At some point, you have to actually pull the trigger, and that's the part that trips a lot of people up. Remember that many things—paint, art on the walls, linens and pillow covers, and other decorative finishes—are very easy to change, and they can make all the difference. Block off a time in your schedule to actually do it, and then commit, because it's quite literally not that serious.

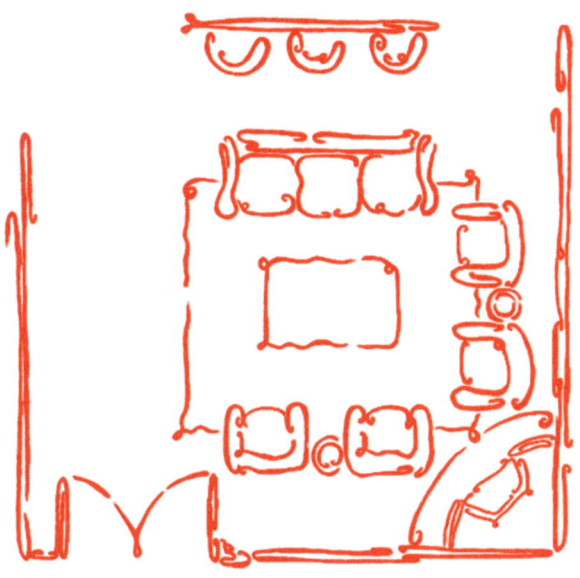

Once the space is created, I think about what it means to take a room from "my everyday home" to "a restaurant-esque place of gathering,"—and, importantly, how I can separate the two. In fact, the ritual of preparing my home for guests is one of my favorite aspects of hosting.

There are certain candles I only break out for guests, pre-set lighting modes for the living and dining rooms, playlists I've curated for dinner parties, and a variety of serving items that only get used when we're having company. There are no real rules about what is for you versus for guests, but I like the automatic whimsy that comes with having special-occasion stuff. And it doesn't necessarily mean these things are fancier: They could be quirkier, more colorful, or have a special story behind them. The point is that finding small ways to go outside what you usually do is an easy way to make your home feel more like an *experience*, without needing to break the bank on themed decor. It's not that I don't feel worthy enough to use my special-occasion items when I'm alone—though I definitely don't have enough patience to clean up all that stuff on a regular basis—I simply view my home as two different entities.

Sometimes people are shy about hosting because it feels too intimate. And I won't gaslight you here; there is definitely a vulnerability about it. I also believe that mentally separating out your home in this way can help ease that anxiety. There is a version of my home that my guests generally never see, or at least, only the closest ones do, and that provides me a layer of protection. I almost always find myself pushing some last-minute cleaning supplies into a closet, or switching out whatever scream-y reality show I was watching for a vibey playlist.

Especially for larger gatherings—where I may not know every guest well—having things set up the way I want *others* to see it helps me feel free to enjoy the party as if I were a guest myself. This means different things for everyone: For me, for example, I always try to have fresh flowers on the table when people walk in the door. For you, it could be using certain dishes, or having freshly cleaned area rugs. It just matters that your home feels ready to welcome in the outside world.

To that end, here are some things I do to prepare for company:

- **DETERMINE THE TIMING.** I like to think about hosting differently based on the season as well as the time of day I'm inviting people over. If we're gathering for a spring brunch, I lean into lighter colors and florals. For a winter cocktail party, it's a lot of darker, richer colors for the decor. It's all about letting the outside environment naturally inform what's happening inside.

- **GET THE LIGHTING RIGHT.** If there is one thing I recommend investing in to take your hosting to the next level, it's lighting you can adjust. That can be dimmer switches, smart bulbs or plugs, or a variety of floor/table/sconce lighting you can turn on in place of a big overhead light. Flattering, warm, and well-diffused lighting will immediately help your guests (and you!) feel at ease. There are few things worse than going to an otherwise-sexy house party and being met with lighting that feels like a dentist's office. Experiment a bit and invest in a few nice taper candles to scatter around the dining area. (Be careful with scented candles; they can irritate allergies or interfere with the taste of food.)

- **FLOWERS, FLOWERS, FLOWERS.** I don't care
if you're stopping for a quick handful of carnations at the
bodega on your way home from work or working with a world-
renowned florist to create custom bouquets. The simple
addition of cut flowers will automatically make any gathering
feel more intentional and the space more friendly. And if
you're on a tight budget, eucalyptus (and other greenery) can
be bought for very little, dries nicely, and can largely serve the
same purpose. (If you're lazy, a few lush hydrangeas literally
always look put-together and impressive.)

- **SET THE MOOD WITH A PLAYLIST.** The right
music can make or break any party, and while many people
love to curate their own playlists for every specific occasion,
there are plenty of Spotify preset playlists that will get the

job done. Just make sure to put something on before people arrive at a low, pleasing volume. Not only does it make for an immediately more enjoyable and cohesive vibe, it also makes people a little less shy about starting conversation.

- **DO A BASKET SWEEP.** Remember when your mom would come to check if your room was clean, and you would immediately start shoving things under your bed and into closets? Any good host should have a few large, relatively chic baskets to carry around and do a quick sweep with, for this exact same purpose. (I'm personally partial to the wicker kind, with lids.) Not everything is going to be perfectly clean right before people arrive, and that is what baskets are for. No shame.

- **PUT FOOD AND DRINKS WHERE YOU WANT PEOPLE TO GATHER.** One of the reasons I always love having a nice assortment of serving dishes—again, thrift shops are key for this!—is so that even the "arrival snacks" can feel like a special moment. I usually have a cluster of little bites on the coffee table, or a cheese board on the dining table, or both, along with a DIY drink station in the kitchen. This takes work off my plate once people arrive, and it creates little zones where people are going to naturally gather. Your setup should naturally direct traffic.

• **SET THE TABLE.** I'm a huge proponent of setting
the table the night before a party. In general, I think a set
table—even a minimally set one—makes a huge difference.
Simple touches—such as layering dinner plates and chargers
(basically a bigger plate that lives under the dinner plate),
selecting a fun tablecloth, tying napkins with ribbon or
string, setting out a bread basket or bottle of wine with a
corkscrew—take minutes, but they have the cumulative effect
of looking like a restaurant-worthy experience that someone
put real thought into.

• **MAKE A BOARD.** I'll often put out a cheese board on the dining table for when people arrive: It's a beautiful display in itself, as well as a natural place for people to gather as they graze. But you don't have to stop at one board. I advocate for multiple boards if you can swing it: charcuterie boards in the living room, dessert boards to come out after the main course, coffee-cream-and-sugar boards, even DIY bagel boards at brunch. There is something simply magical about arranging a bunch of normal ingredients on a big piece of wood. Or, if you don't have a board, use whatever large dish you happen to already have.

The right materials are crucial, yes, but ultimately, setting up the perfect party is about creating a cohesive experience. While not every gathering will have an explicit theme—even I, a person who loves theme parties, simply do not have time for that—thinking in terms of vibes is especially helpful when preparing your space.

Are the flowers and table settings romantic? Maybe find an equally romantic playlist. Does the main course come from a certain country? Find some other touches from that place to sprinkle throughout the party.

Not only do broader themes—as opposed to dedicated holidays, which often necessitate expensive and time-limited decor—help with space transformation, they help guide every individual choice so that planning the event doesn't feel so intimidating. You don't need to overhaul your decor every time a holiday approaches, despite what many home decor influencers would have you believe; but a few things here and there can curate a different experience for each party. This can be as simple as swapping out the colors of taper candles in their holders, or putting seasonal fruit in the centerpiece of your table.

Every space is going to look different, and there are no right or wrong ways to approach decor. The point is to create an experience that allows people to get to know you *and* to feel like themselves when they are visiting. Hosting is the art of thinking just slightly ahead, and the slightest, most budget-friendly efforts—nice lighting, a few fresh flowers, a great playlist—will automatically make you feel like a semi-professional. And while not everything is always going to be perfect, as long as you have a few snacks out for when people arrive, everything else will fall into place.

"My main advice for having people over is that, first, you feel totally confident in your space and in your ability to host people. If you are in a good place—energized and relaxed—then I think that shapes the experience of your guests. My other piece of advice is to think about small details that you can include in the experience that will make your guests feel truly comfortable and special. I think little touches like getting a beverage you know your guest really likes indicate that you really prepared and planned with that guest in mind. I think it also makes people instantly feel cherished and like they belong. When hosts do that for me, I know it really colors my experience and makes me feel very warmly welcomed in their space."

—IFRAH F. AHMED, CHEF AND AUTHOR OF
SOOMAALIYA, A COOKBOOK

Chapter Four

BACK-POCKET RECIPES

THE THING ABOUT HAVING PEOPLE over is that it's always, on some level, about the food. Yes, there can be other reasons for gathering—I love a good game night as much as anyone—but without something to snack or sip on, it just won't get to the transcendent level of a truly great party. That said, just because serving good food is important, it doesn't mean you have to be a great cook. In fact, you don't need to cook much *at all* for the culinary part of your gathering to be memorable. The art of hosting is all about the presentation, and even regular grocery store items can be made to feel special and intentional with just a little bit of prep.

I think making even just a few things always enhances the experience, and often only adds a few minutes of work. For example, the difference between opening up a two-liter soda and making your own homemade strawberry Italian soda? As simple as leaving a bunch of chopped strawberries in a bowl covered with sugar until they naturally create their own syrup, which you then spoon into a glass with some of the berries, fill with ice, and top with club soda. Add a cute paper straw and cocktail napkin, or serve in a fancy stemmed wine glass, and you suddenly have a special-feeling spritz! And you can keep the syrup to use for other things, like topping pancakes or ice cream, or making a summery cocktail.

When I think about cooking for parties, I like to consider what makes the restaurant experience special. Yes, there is the fact that the food often tastes better, but it's also the entire presentation factor that restaurants invest in. It's the fact that everything is done for you and arrives seamlessly, often served in adorable little dishes. The "restaurant experience" comes down to a few tiny details, like

how chefs plate or garnish a dish, or how they break meals into fancy little courses rather than putting everything on the table at once. And when we're making food specifically for hosting, we want to lean into those special details, rather than spend the whole evening in the kitchen, preparing something ultra-complicated.

Having back-pocket recipes is about using *templates* for food, and not as much about the recipes themselves. It's been years since I have cooked most of my food from a recipe, especially if I'm cooking for a large group. And while I sometimes need to follow a recipe closely if I'm trying a totally new dish or cuisine, generally speaking, I've learned the formulas of many, many dishes, and for parties, I stick to what I know. When you're having people over, you want to make things you understand and can easily adjust as needed based on what you have. The mental image we often have of presenting a complicated new dish to your guests isn't just unnecessary; it's often counterproductive to the act of creating a wonderful dining experience. It keeps you stuck in the kitchen, stressed out and hyper-focused on every step of the process.

The other thing to keep in mind about cooking for guests specifically, is that the cocktail hour matters just as much as the main course. We'll cover cocktail hour in detail in the next chapter, but when it comes to the food, the little dishes that people can snack on while moving freely through your space should never be overlooked. Not only is cocktail hour often the best time for conversation—when you're not confined to a single seat at a table—but it's a chance to impress guests with relatively easy recipes that you can often make ahead. Many of the recipes I have here are go-tos for cocktail hour, or dishes I like to make when I serve the entire meal buffet- or tapas-style. And that brings me to my rules for party cooking, starting with the cocktail hour:

- **LET PEOPLE MINGLE.** The "nibble and mingle" portion of the evening should never be overlooked, culinarily. Aside from the social potential it holds, I find that it often lends itself to the easiest recipes: think appetizers such as skewers, dips, spreads, or little fried bites. For my own cocktail hours, I usually like to blend things I've made from scratch with things I bought at the store (like homemade French onion dip with kettle-cooked chips, or fried pickles with a bottled ranch), and I'll usually have some filler items on the table such as olives or nuts. This is also a great time to set out a cheese or charcuterie board, so please refer to my diagram on the anatomy of a board (page 37) for more guidance on that.

- **STAY OUT OF THE KITCHEN.** It can't be stated enough: A dinner party at which you spend most of your time in the kitchen is no dinner party at all. People want to enjoy your food, yes, but they also want to enjoy your company, and you deserve to participate in your own evening, too! What does this mean from a menu perspective? It means focusing on dishes that don't need a lot of last-minute action, especially for the main course. I like things you can cook for hours, and then just keep warm, like pasta sauces, braised meats, or hearty soups. (On that note, French onion soup is always a hit at parties and only requires covering with bread and cheese and sticking under the broiler during the actual party time.) Roasted vegetables, simple salads or slaws, or DIY dishes such as fajitas can also be great. When planning your menu for a party, especially if you're having a lot of guests, make sure that anything that can only be done right before serving—like risotto, nemesis of a chatty dinner party host—to a minimum.

• **LEARN FROM RESTAURANTS.** Why is restaurant food always so good? Well, part of it is the eye-searing quantities of salt, fat, and sugar they use, and that shouldn't be ignored. In my view, cooking for parties should mean a break from your normal health routine and a total disregard for calorie counts. But it also means balancing textures (restaurants love to pair crispy fried food with a creamy sauce or glaze), thoughtful garnishes, and good bread and butter or olive oil on the table for an extra touch. Whenever I'm at a restaurant and have a dish I really love, I take photos of it and write down details in my phone's Notes app, and sometimes I'll even call the restaurant the next day and see if they'll share the recipe. Some of my best go-to dinner party dishes came from restaurant inspiration.

•**FOCUS ON BALANCE.** Just like balancing textures helps achieve that professional feel, every other aspect of your cooking should strive for that same harmony. There are basic rules, like a pinch of salt to enhance sweet foods or a bit of sugar to enhance savory ones, but there are many more ways to achieve balance. A mix of homemade and store-bought dishes helps you focus on what you cook best. Serving fresh vegetables with richer dishes prevents flavors from being overwhelming. The drinks you serve should provide a counterpoint to the food you're enjoying together. Even the timing of the food should feel balanced, with a lighter appetizer preceding a heartier main course, or a lighter dish following a long cocktail hour with plenty of heavy foods.

· **EMBRACE TEMPLATE-BASED COOKING.** In order to get comfortable with cooking for groups, you need to learn basic recipe formulas. This allows you to work better with what you have on hand, and plan menu items that complement each other. For example, if I want to make a complex spritz, I know I'll need something herbaceous or bitter, something sweet, and something sparkly. That can mean a rosemary syrup, grapefruit juice, and club soda, or Campari, muddled strawberries, and sparkling wine. If I want a crowd-pleasing crostini, I'll want something creamy, something salty, and something sweet. I could combine brie, crisped prosciutto, and date syrup; or I could do fresh tomatoes, burrata, and a balsamic reduction. Similarly, for menu planning, you'll want some go-to pairings. If I'm serving a rich pasta, I'll want a fresh salad, and I can play the two off of each other. In summertime, I might want a crab pasta with a sweet corn salad, and in winter I might do a short rib pappardelle with a fennel and citrus slaw.

· **DRAW FROM YOUR LIFE STORY.** When it comes to food that feels like *you*, few things are more helpful than drawing from your own culinary history. Where are you from, what did you grow up eating, where are some places you've been and loved the food? I adore going to someone's house and discovering a dish they ate in childhood, or getting to break out one of my mother's crowd-pleasing recipes at a cocktail party. After a trip to a new place, I love introducing those flavors into my next dinner. (This is, by the way, why spices and other condiments are such great souvenirs to bring back from travel.) The more the food can be reflective of your life, or be the segue into a great story, the more intimate and special your party will feel.

• **DON'T DO IT ALL.** If I've said it once, I've said it a thousand times: Do not put the pressure on yourself to make from scratch every single aspect of the food you serve. You do not need to make handmade pasta or bake your own bread. You don't have to make a homemade dressing for your salad, and a dessert doesn't stop being delicious if you bought it from a bakery instead of spending all afternoon creating it. If you want to make absolutely everything by hand, feel free,

Recipe

From the Kitchen of

Serves ___ Prep Time ___ Cook Time ___ Oven Time ___

Ingredients

Directions,

but do not feel like your party is in any way diminished by not doing so. Instead, select the foods you're most excited about making or feel most comfortable with, and build the menu out from there. The dishes you make will, over time, become your back-pocket recipes; with each passing year, they will make hosting easier and more intuitive.

The recipes that become *your* back-pocket recipes are going to vary, and I've included some of mine in this book to give you an idea. For me, they aren't just recipes that I can make with my eyes closed, they are also dishes that *feel* special without necessarily needing to *be* all that special. As you get more comfortable with hosting, it's nice to start developing your own little book of recipes that feel like your signature set. You don't necessarily need to invent them— and again, they don't even have to be fully homemade—but part of recreating that restaurant experience means having your own vibe and menu. When friends come over again and again, it's nice to hear excitement when they learn you're making a signature dish they love, and it can also help them plan to bring something that complements what you're likely to cook.

I think having go-to cuisines you default to can also be helpful in this regard. In my house, I gravitate toward French, Italian, Sichuan, and Cuban. The former two are cuisines I grew up with, or regions I lived in. The latter two I learned as an adult, but cook frequently enough for myself and my husband that I feel comfortable making them for larger groups. In each cuisine, I have recipes I can easily make ahead of time or adapt to fit the needs of my gathering. Learning the kind of flavor profiles you most enjoy is also helpful: Everything from spice level to acidity to balance of sweet and savory can become recurring themes in the restaurant that is your home. Back-pocket recipes are all about finding your own identity as a host. Even if you're not making everything from scratch, they can still be part of the greater picture you're painting when you have people over.

Cooking for groups is a pretty different experience from cooking for yourself or your immediate family. And sometimes this can add a level of pressure to the process—if nothing else, it means more people to potentially judge your food. But I like to look at it as its own endeavor, and lean into what makes it more fun rather than more complicated. Stretching out the cocktail hour, serving things family-style, making more indulgent meals than you normally would: all of this is part of the beauty that is cooking for others. It's not about impressing everyone with the most daring dish you've made all year; it's about turning your home into a charming little bistro for the evening and getting to decide exactly what's on the menu.

"My advice comes from my Moroccan culture: I always prepare twice as much food as I need, and everyone leaves with Tupperwares of leftovers!"

—JIHANE EL ATIFI, ENTREPRENEUR AND CONSULTANT

Drinks

MINT LEMONADE SPRITZ

SERVES 1

2 sprigs fresh mint, plus more for garnish

Juice of 1 lemon

Simple syrup (dissolve one part sugar in one part water)

Ice

Sparkling water

1 lemon wheel

When I want a good mocktail, I usually want something with citrus. I know this drink is not technically healthful—the simple syrup has plenty of sugar—but there's something about a nice lemony drink that just feels so fresh and reasonable. A sparkling mint lemonade is usually my go-to, though I will often rotate through different herbs such as basil or rosemary. This is just as good for a summertime brunch as it is for a winter cocktail party.

In the bottom of a tall glass, muddle the mint in the lemon juice. Add simple syrup to your desired level of sweetness—I usually start with about a tablespoon. Fill the glass with ice and top with sparkling water. Garnish with more fresh mint and a lemon wheel.

LOIRE VALLEY SPRITZ

SERVES 1

2 ounces Lillet Rosé

1 ounce fresh
grapefruit juice

Ice

2 ounces dry sparkling
wine (preferably a
Loire Valley sparkling
wine)

2 ounces sparkling
water

1 grapefruit wheel

1 sprig rosemary

*Come summertime, I love a good, not-too-sweet spritz, and this one is
a little homage to my first romance novel, set on a vineyard in the Loire
Valley. You can make it with or without booze, and it has a neutral enough
flavor profile to be served with most appetizers.*

Combine the Lillet and grapefruit juice in a wine glass, then fill to the top
with ice. Slowly pour in the sparkling wine and sparkling water (so it doesn't
bubble over!). Garnish with the grapefruit wheel and rosemary.

**Note: To make this spritz virgin, swap out the Lillet for an ounce of simple syrup
(a rosemary-infused simple syrup could be great here), and replace the sparkling wine
with ginger beer.**

TOMATO & PEPPERONCINI MARTINI

SERVES 1

4 sweet cherry tomatoes

Simple syrup (optional)

2½ ounces good-quality vodka

½ ounce white balsamic vinegar

½ ounce pepperoncini brine

Freshly cracked black pepper

1 pepperoncini, for garnish

I love a good dirty martini. But sometimes I get a little tired of the same old olive flavor and want to mix it up. This martini is a crowd-pleaser and still has all the brininess of a good dirty martini, with a bit more complexity and a hint of sweetness. It's the ultimate summer sipper. Note that you will need a cocktail shaker and a chilled martini glass for this one.

Muddle 3 of the sweet cherry tomatoes in the bottom of your cocktail shaker. If you like your drink a bit on the sweet side, add a splash of simple syrup here. Fill the cocktail shaker with ice and add the vodka, vinegar, and brine. Shake well for at least 30 seconds. Strain into a chilled martini glass and top with black pepper. Thread the remaining cherry tomato and pepperoncini on a cocktail skewer and garnish the drink with the skewer.

Food

CACIO E PEPE FRIED OLIVES

MAKES 2 CUPS

Oil for deep-frying (such as canola or peanut oil)

16 ounces pitted castelvetrano olives (at least one jar), drained

2 cups all-purpose flour

2 eggs, beaten

2 cups panko crumbs

Pecorino cheese, freshly grated

Freshly cracked black pepper

If there is one appetizer I make more than any other, it's fried olives. These are always a hit (provided the guests enjoy olives, which, luckily, most of mine do). They seem so fancy considering how easy they are to assemble. Plus, adding the phrase "cacio e pepe" to basically anything automatically makes it so much more exciting.

Heat a few inches of oil in a frying-safe pot over medium-high heat, to roughly 350°F. Line a dish with paper towels for draining the fried olives.

Pat the olives dry.

Set up a breading station with three bowls: one with the flour, one with the eggs, and one with panko crumbs. Working in small batches, toss some olives in the flour until lightly coated (do not season the flour, as this dish is already very salty). Transfer the floured olives into the bowl with the beaten eggs, and toss them until coated. From there, toss the egged olives in the panko crumbs.

Add a batch of breaded olives to the hot oil, turning one or two times until golden brown on all sides, about 3 minutes total. Transfer the fried olives to the paper towel–lined dish. Continue to fry in batches until you have the amount you want.

While still hot, toss the fried olives in a bowl with the grated pecorino and freshly cracked pepper until lightly seasoned. Transfer them to a serving dish and top with a little more cheese and pepper. Voilà!

TINNED FISH AND WHITE BEAN DIP

SERVES 8

2 (7-ounce) cans fish (I like bonito, smoked trout, or just a garden-variety canned tuna)

1 (15.5-ounce) can small white beans (navy or cannellini)

Several sprigs of dill, finely chopped, plus more for garnish

Several sprigs of parsley, finely chopped, plus more for garnish

Several chive stems, finely chopped, plus more for garnish

½ yellow onion, finely diced

Juice of 1 large lemon

Pinch of sugar

Kosher salt and freshly cracked black pepper

Several glugs of good-quality olive oil

Toasted bread, cucumber rounds, lettuce cups, or crackers, for serving

I'd like to pretend that I'm above a trend, but as someone who's been eating canned fish forever as a great, easy protein source, I love that it has recently become a chic ingredient. "Tinned fish" is just another name for it, but it does add an air of sophistication to what is ultimately a very basic food. Here's one of my favorite easy appetizers that utilizes it.

If using fish packed in water, drain it before emptying both cans into a large bowl. Lightly shred the fish with a fork. Add the white beans, dill, parsley, chives, onion, lemon juice, and sugar. Add salt and pepper to taste. How much salt you need will depend on whether or not the canned fish is salted. Add the olive oil. The quantity will depend on whether your fish was packed in oil or water. Stir gently to combine, adding more oil as necessary to get a nice, spreadable consistency. Adjust the seasoning to taste. Top with more fresh herbs and serve with something to dip.

MY FAMOUS WHITE BOLOGNESE

SERVES 4

2 tablespoons olive oil, plus more as needed

4 ounces pancetta, diced

1½ pounds ground meat (I like a mix of beef and lamb)

Kosher salt and freshly cracked black pepper

1 cup finely diced carrot

1 cup finely diced celery

1 cup finely diced onion

1 large sprig of rosemary

1 large sprig of thyme

1 bay leaf

4 garlic cloves, minced

1 glass (about 6 ounces) dry white wine

1 (32-ounce) box high-quality unsalted chicken stock

Large pinch of sugar

1 (16-ounce) box chunky pasta (I like paccheri or pappardelle)

1 cup freshly grated Parmesan cheese, plus more for garnish

1 cup heavy cream

This is my go-to pasta dish for parties because it's my husband's favorite, it's easy to make ahead, and it's just unique enough to feel more impressive than it is. You can even make the sauce the night before and just heat it up the day of the party when you cook off the pasta.

In a large, heavy pot, heat the olive oil over medium-high heat. Add the pancetta and sauté until the pieces are nice and crispy. Remove the pancetta with a slotted spoon and set aside on a paper towel–lined plate, keeping the oil in the pot.

Add the ground meat to the pot and season with a healthy pinch of salt and several cracks of pepper. Cook for a few minutes over medium-high heat until you get good caramelization on the outside of the meat, taking care not to overcook. With a slotted spoon, transfer the meat to the plate with the pancetta, once again keeping the oil in your pot. Add another glug of olive oil, if needed, to fully coat the bottom of the pot.

Add the carrot, celery, and onion to the pot, along with the rosemary, thyme, and bay leaf. Lower the heat to medium and cook until the onions have just started to soften, a few minutes. Add the garlic and continue to cook until the onions are translucent and the carrots and celery have begun to soften, at least 10 minutes more. Stir frequently so the vegetables do not burn.

Add the wine and stir well to deglaze the pot. Cook until the liquid has mostly evaporated.

Return the meat and pancetta to the pot. Add the stock and a large pinch of sugar. Bring to a boil, then turn the heat low. Simmer over low heat until the liquid has reduced by at least two-thirds, then remove the herbs from the pot and discard.

While the sauce simmers, cook the pasta in boiling salted water according to the package instructions until just before it reaches an al dente texture. Drain the noodles, reserving a bit of the pasta water for the sauce.

Once the sauce has reduced, stir in the Parmesan and cream. Season with salt and pepper to taste.

Add the pasta to the sauce, stirring until the sauce begins to thicken and adhere to the noodles, adding the reserved pasta water as needed to help the sauce attain the perfect, saucy consistency. Serve in bowls topped with plenty of freshly grated Parmesan.

HARISSA CRISPY POTATOES

SERVES 4

4 russet potatoes, peeled and cut into small, equal-size cubes

½ cup all-purpose flour

½ cup olive oil, plus more as needed

4 garlic cloves, finely minced or crushed

3 tablespoons harissa paste

Kosher salt

Lemon wedges, for serving

Fresh cilantro leaves, roughly chopped, for garnish

Crispy potatoes are one of my go-to sides, not just because they're insanely easy and versatile, but because they're one of those foods that always elevates a meal to restaurant quality. This is one of my favorite template recipes for when I'm hosting! I frequently change up what I toss the potatoes in when they come out of the oven (Old Bay seasoning, lemon pepper, and garlic and herb butter are some favorites), but I'm always a fan of a little spice, so here is my recipe for the harissa variation!

Preheat the oven to 425°F.

Add the potatoes to a pot of salted water, bring to a boil, and boil until fork-tender, about 12 minutes. The time will vary depending on the size of your potato cubes. Drain the potatoes in a colander.

Pour the olive oil onto a large baking sheet and place in the oven to preheat until sizzling hot, at least 5 minutes.

Add the flour to the potatoes in the colander and toss to coat. Remove the baking sheet from the oven and carefully transfer the potatoes to the hot baking sheet and arrange so each piece is flat in the oil.

Bake until crispy and golden brown on each side, flipping once halfway through. Depending on your oven and the size of your potatoes, this generally takes about 15 minutes per side. In the last few minutes of baking, add the garlic and spread it evenly around your potatoes so it roasts slightly but doesn't burn.

Once the potatoes are fully crisp, transfer them to a bowl and toss with the harissa and salt to taste. Serve with lemon wedges on the side and fresh cilantro sprinkled over top.

RESTAURANT-WORTHY BRUSSELS SPROUTS

SERVES 4

2 pounds brussels sprouts, trimmed and halved

2 tablespoons olive oil

Generous pinch each of kosher salt and freshly cracked black pepper

¼ cup unsalted butter

2 tablespoons soy sauce

2 tablespoons maple syrup

1 tablespoon balsamic vinegar

Crushed red pepper flakes

1 scallion, trimmed and thinly sliced on the diagonal, for garnish

Whenever you order brussels sprouts at a restaurant, you likely wonder why the ones you make at home never taste as good. (For years, I asked myself the same question.) The answer is heat! They dry those little suckers out well past what seems reasonable, because brussels sprouts are full of water, and to achieve that delightful crispiness—especially to preserve it once they are tossed in a glaze—you need them to be bone-dry. Here is my go-to version of the dish.

Preheat the oven to 475°F.

In a large bowl, toss the brussels sprouts in the olive oil until lightly coated. Season with salt and pepper. Arrange the brussels sprouts cut-side down on a baking sheet in an even layer, making sure that each half is fully in contact with the sheet (don't crowd them!).

Roast the brussels sprouts for about 25 minutes, flipping them once halfway through. The time is approximate because every oven is different, and the goal is to get them as dried-out and crispy as possible without burning them.

Turn the oven off and leave them in there, so they can continue to dry out while the temperature comes down slightly, about 5 minutes.

While the brussels sprouts are roasting, make the glaze: Melt the butter and combine it with the soy sauce, maple syrup, balsamic vinegar, and a few pinches of the crushed red pepper flakes.

Remove the brussels sprouts from the oven and let cool until they are warm but not hot (too hot, and the glaze will ruin the crispiness). Toss the sprouts in the glaze until well coated, transfer to a serving dish, and garnish with scallions.

WHIPPED LEMON MOUSSE

SERVES 4

1 cup heavy
cream

2 tablespoons
confectioners' sugar

Kosher salt

½ cup lemon curd

Zest of 1 lemon

Juice of ½ lemon

Anyone who knows me knows that I can't bake to save my life; I generally never make dessert myself. But sometimes I like making the meal from start to finish, and this not-quite-from-scratch lemon "mousse" is easy and delicious. Serve by itself, with fresh berries, or even on top of a slice of pound cake.

In a large, chilled bowl, whip the cream, sugar, and a pinch of salt until the cream forms stiff peaks.

In a separate bowl, combine the lemon curd, half of the zest, and the lemon juice. Gently fold the whipped cream into the lemon curd mixture until combined. Transfer to serving bowls and top with the remaining lemon zest.

"Discuss the menu with your guests ahead of time. I know some hostesses prefer dinner party menus to be a surprise, but I just don't operate that way. Partially because this way I can sus out any allergies/aversions, but also because it gives me *and* my guests something to look forward to. I'm not a spontaneous girlie; I always, always need specific plans on my calendar for my own mental health. And I adore baking for people, so knowing they are as excited as I am to eat a cake I'm making makes me so happy."

—HOLLY TRANTHAM, CREATIVE DIRECTOR

Chapter Five

COCKTAIL
(OR MOCKTAIL)

HOUR,
A SACRED
MOMENT

IF THERE IS ONE SHOW I have watched and loved more than any other, it is *Mad Men*. The classic series follows the lives of advertising executives in 1960s New York City. It is my comfort show, my annual rewatch, and it likely shaped my own personal style and sensibilities in ways I'll never fully know. (During its initial airing, I was also dating a creative director at an ad agency quite a few years older than me, something that felt deeply chic to me at the time. Hope he's doing well!)

Over the years, the show has taken on different meanings to me, and each new viewing teases out nuances that demand a maturity that I didn't have on first watch. But one thing that has become glaringly obvious to me is just how much alcohol is glamorized, and how much the series's cautionary tale around alcohol abuse could easily be lost on someone who is only engaging with the show on a surface level. But when the show initially aired in 2007, much ink was spilled on how much *Mad Men* impacted contemporary culture, and one of those impacts was reviving a seemingly dormant interest in the cocktail party. The intimate gatherings looked so lovely on the show: stylish mid-century apartments, little appetizers on skewers, and perpetually full buckets of ice chilling on the sideboard. Everyone was so fashionable, and especially in the early seasons, the show looked like a fantasy version of the lives our parents or grandparents might have been living, depending on the age of the viewer. (For my part, my late grandmother really *was* that glamorous, with her perfect outfits and expertly appointed homes, down to the frosted pink highball glasses I inherited from her.)

Although the show took great pains to portray the darkness of the era, the cost hidden behind a superficially perfect world, the social impact it had on viewers mostly centered on the fabulousness. For my part, in combination with the party-hosting upbringing I received, it felt like a siren call: Eighteen-year-old Chelsea decided that she, too, would have fabulous cocktail parties, and the more fully realized they were, the more she would feel like a grown-up.

It is no secret, however, that younger generations are having a reckoning with alcohol. Millennials and gen Z-ers drink much less than their parents—according to a 2023 Gallup poll, about 62 percent of adults under the age of thirty-five drink now, down from 72 percent only two decades ago—and when they *do* drink, it's in lower quantities. Even as someone who enjoys a good dirty martini or Campari spritz, I have become much more aware of the role alcohol can play in our society, and how insidious it can become in our lives—especially for women, toward whom alcohol is so aggressively marketed as a reward. Most of us millennials were raised by the boomer generation, and it's undeniable that older generations' views on substance use were and are very different. It was normalized in all of the ways we are now taught to be skeptical of: It was a right, it was something to be seamlessly integrated into all aspects of life, and if you didn't get on board, you were bringing the whole room down.

While our parents' generation went much too far with drinking culture, they *did* often use it as a tool for social gatherings. And it's undeniable that as the generations progress, we are socializing less and less. (In fact, gen Z reports itself as being the *most* isolated generation for their age group: the people of other eras were going out and seeing friends quite a bit more in their early- to mid-twenties.*) Today, we are forming fewer connections, taking less time for our social lives, and—if we have children—making the children increasingly the focus of our lives to the exclusion of important adult relationships.

For all their faults, boomers (and the generations before them) had people over more, and this seems to have been a trend regardless of income level. Younger people who have the financial means to be socializing simply aren't doing it as much. I think part of this may be due to the fact that, culturally, socialization still remains very much tied to the consumption of alcohol.

Both in my own life and in how I view the world around me, I think the truth lies somewhere in the middle. We are right to reject a social landscape that still relies so heavily on drinking—again, a relic from a generation with a much less healthy relationship to the substance—but we are not right to assume that these two things cannot be decoupled. When one goes to countries with much more robust cultures of community, we can see just how much socializing happens compared to the average life of an American. (Spend a single day in Spain, for example, and you will see people of all ages at all hours gathered at outdoor cafes, in town squares, at parks, in each other's homes: Spaniards are never not having a yap around a table!) But I agree with our younger generation that the implicit necessity of alcohol for gathering isn't just unhealthy

* "Gen-Z, The Lonliness Epidemic and the Unifying Power of Brands," by Kian Bakhtiari, Forbes Magazine, July 28, 2023, https://www.forbes.com/sites/kianbakhtiari/2023/07/28/gen-z-the-loneliness-epidemic-and-the-unifying-power-of-brands/.

physically; it also takes a serious social toll on the people who participate. "Getting together for drinks" in the United States can make non-drinkers feel uncomfortable, often requires a budget commitment—cocktails are pricey!—and opens up the risk of seriously inappropriate behavior.

I do believe the concept of the cocktail hour—the aperitif, as it is known in France—is a marvelous one. At more formal dinner parties, it's always my favorite part, if only because of the freedom of movement and conversation it provides. In an ideal world, we're gathered around in the fading early-evening light, snacking on a delightful assortment of finger foods, and giddy with the knowledge that the evening is just beginning. When I lived in France, and whenever my husband and I are there now, one of my absolute favorite things is how much of a cultural staple the aperitif is. It doesn't matter what everyone was off doing during the day, or what the plans for dinner are—come 7 p.m., someone is going to put out a couple of snacks and start the conversation.

During the aperitif, I've often opted for a soda over a glass of wine, and it has never dampened the experience. And I realize that this is because, unlike the drink-to-be-drunk culture often encouraged in the States, the point isn't the drink itself—it's the company. You can have a beautiful conversation in the magic-hour light just as effectively with a lemonade as with an Aperol spritz.

While my husband and I don't always honor that hour in our home when it's just the two of us—frankly, I don't want to deal with the dishes—I do try to cultivate the experience as often as possible. Every time we're having out-of-town guests, for example, we always make it happen, and my dinner parties never begin without at least an hour-long stretch of pre-dinner mingling. Sometimes, we'll invite people over for a cocktail hour before we head out to a restaurant, or we'll do a late-afternoon regroup to socialize after a daytime outing. As we typically eat dinner late in my house, it aligns well with our schedule, and, regardless of what is in our glasses, it always makes a day feel so much richer.

If you, too, would like to embrace the spirit of cocktail hour (with or without actual spirits), here are a few items you might want. As it pertains to any kind of home goods or serving ware, I *highly recommend* shopping at thrift stores. Not only are the items often much more unique and beautiful, they are also a fraction of the price of new things. Most of my best pieces were purchased at thrift stores, and I'm always on the lookout for more.

TO SERVE

- A nice, oversize platter or board for arranging snacks, making a charcuterie board, or carrying things into another room

- Cocktail napkins (I prefer fabric napkins generally, but often opt for paper with larger groups)

- A variety of glasses such as:

  - Highball

  - Coupe

  - Rocks

  - Wine glass

- A few different bowls for serving (you can always use regular bowls, but I think this is a fun time to get pieces in unique colors/dimensions)

- Toothpicks

- A bucket or large bowl for ice

TO DRINK

I will often get special ingredients for a drink, but these are some things I generally have on hand at all times:

- Sparkling wine
- Seltzer
- Bitters
- Rosé
- Ginger beer
- Campari
- Fresh citrus
- Simple syrup

TO EAT

Similarly, while I will sometimes buy items specifically for cocktail hour, this is what I always have around:

- Mixed nuts
- Kettle chips
- Dry sausage
- Cheese
- Jarred olives
- Canned fish
- Water crackers

For hosting your cocktail hour, the goal is to minimize work on your part and maximize your ability to enjoy the evening. This means snacks are never complicated (the most I'll usually do for a cocktail hour is make a quick dip to serve with crackers, or maybe assemble some skewers), and the drinks aren't either. I set up a beverage station where people can serve themselves, sometimes with a main "signature" drink ready in a large batch. A drink station allows people to serve themselves at their own pace, too. Having a nice mix of nonalcoholic options on offer is a great way to make your evening inclusive and reduce the focus on inebriation for its own sake—bonus points if there is a special zero-proof mixed drink.

Although these informal gatherings are great any time of year, I think the magic of cocktail hour comes alive in the spring and summer. Not only is the sun out for much longer—therefore putting cocktail hour during the most flattering evening light—there is also a renewed energy for casual socialization, a desire to linger in the small moments.

This summer, I recommend starting a little ritual, even if just with the people in your own home: Once or twice a week, at an appointed time of day, set out a casual little cocktail hour with the food and drinks you love, and make a point to mingle. Put your phone away, slow down a bit, and rejoice in the fact that you don't need a big, over-the-top dinner party to enjoy each other's company.

Mad Men may have had many impacts on our culture, for good and bad, but where the show definitely succeeded was in creating nostalgia for a time when hosting was simply more common. The luxury and glamour of those mid-century New York City parties may have been much too tied to alcohol, but in our own lives, we can acknowledge that we simply don't need alcohol as an excuse or a catalyst to get together and celebrate in a more casual, spontaneous way. We can put on a nice outfit, assemble a great playlist, and gather around a spread of finger foods for no reason at all, and we don't have to wait for the cultural impetus of another TV phenomenon in order to do it.

"Always set up the bar area fully before company arrives. I always find myself needing that extra ten to fifteen minutes of crucial prep/cooking time while people busy themselves making a drink and garnishing their beverage of choice. (And always grab an extra bag of ice!) But most importantly, enjoy yourself and don't stress. You should have fun and lean into what the hangout is all about: Spending time with those you love."

—LAUREN VER HAGE, DESIGNER

Chapter Six

THE
BASIC
DINNER
PARTY

THIS WOULD SIMPLY NOT BE a hosting book without a chapter on the almighty dinner party. At this point in my life, I have hosted hundreds, and I have made plenty of mistakes, but only once did things go so wrong that I ended up having to order a pizza. (It turns out, if you forget about a sauce cooking on the stovetop while playing a board game for an hour, you burn it.) I have also picked up countless tricks and good habits along the way and have gotten so efficient that I regularly host dinner parties on weeknights with minimal stress and zero impact on my work.

But the most important thing I've learned when hosting dinner parties is to set them up so that *you (the host) actually get to enjoy the dinner, too.* I used to think that throwing grown-up parties was about spending the whole time serving everyone else. Now I know that if you don't get to enjoy your party, it's—quite frankly—a waste of time and money.

But I also understand why a lot of people never even bother to undertake throwing a dinner party, let alone attempt to *enjoy* throwing them. A dinner party can feel incredibly intimidating. In sitcoms and movies, dinner parties are portrayed as stressful events, where you invite over your boss and panic while making a soufflé. (Side note: I have also been to countless dinner parties, and never once did someone make a soufflé. Could this be the result of effective anti-soufflé propaganda?) I get it. Hosting a dinner party might not seem particularly fun from the outside, and I would be lying if I didn't admit that, they *can* become much more trouble than they're worth. But it's time to reclaim dinner parties, and I assure you that you can throw them—and have fun doing it.

First, I want to reassure everyone that a well-executed dinner party is indeed very cool. They do not have to be stuffy, and they can take any shape that feels authentic or inspiring. But that means planning thoughtfully so your party can be a reflection of yourself and what *you* think a dinner party should be.

To that end, I have a five-step process I follow for planning dinner parties, especially for special occasions. For a more casual evening with close friends we have by regularly, I may not go all out like this. But if you're just starting out, this method is a foolproof way to ensure that you're not overwhelmed in the process.

1. PLANNING AND INVITING

For me, a proper dinner party always starts with an invitation. Sometimes it's actual paper, sometimes it's a Paperless Post, sometimes it's just a good old Google Calendar invite. But I use invitations to set up the parameters, decide on a theme, and start to sketch out my menu. I put all of the relevant information in the invite and will usually inform people what they can bring if they would like to (though I do always specify that their presence is more than enough—which it is!). RSVPs are also a great time to gather information such as dietary restrictions or preferences and to set expectations, like whether shoes will be allowed to remain on, or if there is a dress code. I recommend sending your invites at least two weeks in advance of the event, especially because as we get older, schedules can be more difficult to coordinate, and you'll be able to set your menu (and therefore your shopping list) no less than a week ahead of time.

It's worth starting small, especially if you're newer to hosting. I rarely host seated dinner parties for more than six people, because my table can't accommodate much more than that. But even if you are hosting a more informal buffet-style meal, remember that chaos increases exponentially with more guests. Six and under is a great beginner number, and scaling up as you get more comfortable is a nice way to ease into larger groups.

2. SHOPPING AND PREPPING

I like to do my shopping two to three days in advance of the party, so any food or drink prep can happen the night before. I religiously create grocery lists and always do a thorough scan of my kitchen to know what I have before I buy more. (By the way, it's perfectly okay to base some of your dinner party menu on using what you already have; you don't have to serve a fancy new dish for it to be party-worthy.) I do a mix of premade and homemade, like making a sauce from scratch but using boxed pasta. Or, I'll cook all of the main course, but pick up some appetizers from the prepared-foods section of my grocery store. By relieving the pressure to make everything yourself, you not only get to enjoy your event more, but you also get to focus on the things you make really well, rather than trying to do it all. I usually have a signature drink for my dinner parties, and I'll often make something that people can choose to spike or leave virgin.

When planning menus, I strategically choose things that can be made in advance as much as possible. That can mean prep, like dicing vegetables or breading things I plan to fry, full-on assembly such as putting together my signature drink base, making dips, or tossing a salad together (without dressing it yet). The less I have to do the day of the party, the better.

3. CLEANING AND SETTING UP

The night before a party is all about cleaning. I spend a few hours the eve of any dinner party on food and apartment prep. Unless you have the day off, this is really the only way to do it and maintain your sanity. I like to set my table fully (especially if it's an elaborate tablescape), clean the living spaces, put out serving platters or water pitchers, prep the drink station, and hang any decorations I might have for the occasion. Basically, when I go to bed the night before, I like to know that *almost* everything is ready, and all I need to focus on day-of is the cooking that couldn't happen the night before.

4. PUTTING IT ALL TOGETHER

My dinner parties will often start around 7:30 p.m., which can be slightly late for Americans, but it is a compromise from my prefer-ence, which is to eat like the Spaniards do, at 10 p.m. I also work 9 a.m. to 5 p.m. most days, so that 7:30 call time gives me at least two hours after work to finish everything, and I always need it. There is cooking that can't take place ahead of time, setting out the appetizers, fully stocking the drink station, lighting the candles, cueing the music, and putting on a cute outfit.

I generally shy away from any dishes that require me to be in the kitchen for more than a few minutes at a time, or anything that I'm not yet confident in making. It's not that I don't like to experiment, I just don't prefer to experiment at a time when I'd risk missing my own party and wasting a bunch of money on several servings of inedible food. This pre-arrival time is about taking care of the little things so that you can curate the flow of the evening more effectively. This might mean getting out board games you might like to play or pulling a book from your shelves that you've been meaning to recommend to a friend.

5. ENJOYING THE SHOW

Once people arrive, it's time to just vibe. This is the point at which you stop worrying if everything is perfect, stop apologizing for mistakes, and stop focusing on every little detail in service of the bigger picture. This is where having a partner or cohost comes in very handy; my husband is very good at making sure that I'm actually participating in the conversation and getting served enough food. But you should also check in frequently with yourself: Are you stressing about something objectively unimportant? Are you able to actually join your guests? Are you spending the whole time in the kitchen? Learning to relax and lean into the experience you've created is a skill—trust me, I've lost many evenings to my own irritating internal monologue—but it is the most important part of the entire process.

This might sound counterintuitive to the concept of hosting others, but a key element to getting comfortable with being a dinner party hostess is making *your* preferences known. It's a lot easier to throw a dinner if you're okay with telling guests what they can bring or letting them know when you're ready to send them home and go to bed. A lot of us weren't raised to truly feel like the masters of our own domain, especially as women, and it can go against our nature to direct people. But having a firm-but-gentle hand around whether that's telling guests if they can serve themselves another drink, announcing when dinner is ready, or asking attendees to be a little quieter after a certain hour helps *them* feel more comfortable, because it helps them be good guests. Guests don't want to feel like they're unintentionally embarrassing themselves, so if you're the type of host who wants shoes off even for a formal dinner, tell them! Don't let guests accidentally violate your preferences and just stare at their feet awkwardly for the entire dinner. Hosting is first and foremost about enjoying one another's company, and setting some basic guidelines helps everyone do that more effortlessly.

Similarly, remember that the flaws that seem very obvious to you—the dust bunny in the corner, the slightly burnt pie crust, the mismatched plates—likely won't even register to your guests. Drawing attention to things you don't like in your home is a very common reflex for many us, especially women, and I have definitely been guilty of the practice many times—but it's also the easiest way to guarantee that people *will* actually remember what you're hoping they don't notice.

I couldn't begin to count the number of dinner parties I've attended, and I've frankly always had a wonderful time. Sure, there have been some awkward fights between the host couple—though honestly, those always make for compelling conversation on the way home—but overall, I remember the joys much more than any "mistakes."

As a guest, I love the coziness of being invited into a friend's home and rarely, if ever, focus on the details. And by remembering how I view a party from the other (guest) side, I always give myself a little more grace when I am hosting. I still laugh thinking about the night I ruined a sauce and had to order pizza: I had my guests gather around the pot in the kitchen, making them taste it to get their second (and third, and fourth) opinions. I was so panicked in the moment, my anxiety mounting with each grimace on a friend's face that indicated how unsalvageable the sauce actually was.

This memory used to feel embarrassing, but now it makes me feel warm, because I know my guests will remember the laughter as we laid the doomed sauce to rest, and our wonderful conversation while passing around the greasy pizza boxes, our faces lit by candlelight and the music gently playing around us. The imperfections are what ultimately makes the act of entertaining feel more human and more full of life.

"My most helpful (and boring, tbh) tip for having people over is to do everything you can ahead of time! Set the table, including your serving dishes, and make whatever you can the day before. It'll help you be more relaxed and actually enjoy yourself! My runner-up tip is to have cute cocktail napkins out with drinks and snacks; it always makes people think you have it all together."

—HEATHER BRENNAN, PROJECT MANAGER

Chapter Seven

THE
(PLATONIC)
ADULT
SLEEPOVER

IF THERE IS ONE MAJOR criticism I have for our society (at least, as it pertains to relationships), it's how much we prioritize romantic relationships at the expense of platonic ones. We are constantly neglecting friendships and reserving our most dedicated effort for other types of connections in our life. Friends are often treated as an afterthought, as though their continuity and intensity are foregone conclusions. But to achieve real, lasting closeness with people to whom you are neither bound by the commitment of marriage nor the obligation of family is an important skill, and a noble goal.

This devaluing of friends has also put immense pressure on our romantic partners to meet our every need—a systemic issue that has led to, among other things, a rising epidemic of male loneliness.* Notice how we reserve so many of life's joys for the person we're sleeping with: We save our most creative and thoughtful selves for our partners, plan trips and curate date nights, show up for them in ways that create softness around the sharp edges of their lives. Many of the most fundamental acts of love and intimacy are reserved for them and, at least in my experience, that often includes overnight stays.

If you ask the average adult, they'll agree that spending the night at someone's house is utterly normal—as long as you're also sleeping with them. You might have overnights with families or trips with larger friend groups, but if you're heading somewhere in

---

* "The State of American Friendship: Change, Challenges, and Loss: Findings from the May 2021 American Perspectives Survey," by Daniel A. Cox, Survey Center on American Life, June 8, 2021, https://www.americansurveycenter.org/research/the-state-of-american-friendship-change-challenges-and-loss/.

your own city for more than a few hours, it's generally because this is a person you're dating, or at least hooking up with. And don't get me wrong, I've had plenty of that kind of sleepover, and they can be great. (Although frankly, they can also be horrible!) The point is, we have a very clear idea in our mind of what a "sleepover" is, and unless it's with someone you found on Tinder, it's generally considered to be an activity for children.

I'm always thinking of ways to make my adult life feel more magical, and much of that requires looking back to childhood. Sleepovers had a thrilling permissiveness to them, a promise that the fun did not have to end. They always elicited the best and most

intimate conversations, the late-night confessions, whispered under the dimmest light you could get away with having on. There was sneaking down to the kitchen for a midnight snack, falling asleep delirious from laughter, and knowing that you would wake up in the morning to a shared breakfast with one of the people you loved most in the world. (Especially for those whose houses were generally devoid of prepackaged foods—like mine was—it also meant a hedonistic descent into everything from Pop-Tarts to Doritos to Mountain Dew.) Sleepovers *are* childlike, and that's what makes them so wonderful as an adult.

All that is to say I am a big proponent of the platonic adult sleepover, and I try to have them as often as possible, usually coinciding with my husband's work or personal travel. In addition to our out-of-town guests, who generally breeze through a few times per quarter, I will host a woman from my own city about once every other month.

At my sleepovers, there is always a theme, a planned menu, and activities that require nothing more than being in pajamas on the couch, as well as the full-bodied joy of knowing no one has to schlep themselves home after dinner. These sleepovers can be a reprieve especially for the moms in my life, who relish an overnight getaway that doesn't require actual travel (or the cost of a hotel room). They can be excellent bonding moments for friends whose closeness is finally starting to tip over into the "lifelong" category, and they're also one of my favorite ways to catch up with the friends I've had since childhood. In general, as relatively few adults tend to have platonic sleepovers, they always have a festive specialness and make otherwise-mundane activities—even something as simple as watching a movie—feel new and exciting.

I should say up front before we get into details that these overnights do, of course, require a level of privilege. It's helpful (though not necessary) to have a guest room. Not having children gives me ample time to prepare, and I do have a husband who leaves town frequently enough to make overnight hosting easier in a relatively small apartment. But in my experience, many more people *could* be hosting sleepovers who aren't, especially those who live in much larger spaces than I do (which, as a Manhattanite, is basically everyone).

When children spend the night together, their parents could join them. When a friend is having a particularly rough week, you could make it better by curating a little staycation. There's no reason a movie night has to end with someone going home, at least not every time. But there is a kind of firewall in all of our brains: Past a certain age, this particular kind of intimacy is reserved for romantic partners (or, at least, physical ones). To have grown-ups stay the night if they are not coming from out of town is just a little weird.

The weirdness, though, *is* the fabulousness. And it's not just about the late-night gossip or joy of watching movies together in your pajamas as an adult. It's an act of love that doesn't also require an act of physicality, that places a high level of importance on platonic relationships because they, too, are worth celebrating. My platonic sleepovers are some of my favorite things in life, and I firmly believe that everyone should try one at least once.

Here is my seven-step guide to throwing an adult platonic sleepover in your own home.

Step 1

SCHEDULE AHEAD OF TIME

If you want to get two working adults together (especially working parents), you are going to have to get used to scheduling your plans way ahead of time. I use Google Calendar, and I generally send the invite with all the relevant details at least a few weeks ahead, after we agree on a date. (Side note: This is yet another thing we tend to only reserve for our romantic partners—going out of our way to make dates. Friends also deserve to be a part of your monthly calendar.)

Step 2

CREATE A GUEST SPACE
YOU'D WANT TO STAY IN

This is where living in a bigger space is really helpful, but with the right attention to detail, even a living room can be made into a cozy guest suite. I think the most important things to consider here are:

- Comfortable, clean bedding (I also like things such as mattress toppers or other adjustments if you're turning a couch into a bed)

- Fresh towels and washcloths for their shower, plus a robe and slippers if you can swing it

- Basic shower supplies (these will likely live in the bathroom, but make sure shampoo, face wash, body soap, and so on are all stocked)

- A pitcher of water and a glass so they don't have to get up in the middle of the night

- A space to place their bag/affairs

- At least one night-light: to create a cozy sleep space, you need more than just the big light overhead

- Free outlets for them to charge their belongings (an extra charger, if you have one, is also a great touch)

Step 3

PREPARE A GUEST BASKET

I think a guest basket is one of the most low-effort, high-reward touches you can add to your hosting arsenal. For mine, I have a cute little woven basket in which I place the following:

- Cough drops
- Hand sanitizer
- Tampons/pads
- Face mist
- Lotion
- Protein bar

Step 4

PLAN OUT A THEME

To add to the whimsy of the evening, I like to create a theme that lends itself to the sleepover vibe. I coordinate food and drinks, activities, and entertainment around the theme. Some of my favorites:

- Rom-com night
- Home-spa day (sometimes all you want is to do an indulgent beauty ritual while gossiping)
- Witchy vibes
- Mamma Mia (I love this in summer: Greek food, ABBA music, a re-watch of the movies)
- Marie Antoinette

Step 5

PLAN SLEEPOVER-
FRIENDLY ACTIVITIES

Basically, this includes anything that doesn't require you to leave your couch or change out of pajamas. I like:

- Beauty treatments
- Card games
- Crafting

- Puzzles
- Tarot/ astrology

- Movies (obviously)
- Adult coloring books

Step 6

BUILD A LOW-KEY MENU

While I do sometimes love to cook actual meals for sleepovers, between the couch-bound energy and the goal to relax myself, I will often end up with a mix of store-bought (or ordered) foods and some homemade items. I'll often make a spread of homemade appetizers and then order takeout, or I'll assemble some of my favorite premade snacks, followed by an easy dinner I can make ahead of time and pop in the oven (like a baked mac and cheese).

Step 7

GET YOUR LOUNGEWEAR READY

If there's one thing I believe that is crucial to a good adult sleepover, it's the proper attire. This is the time to break out your most adorable loungewear or, depending on your vibe, relish a friendship that allows you to hang out in a shredded old T-shirt. I personally prefer the former, if only because I so rarely have an occasion to show off my cute pajamas, but whichever you choose, know this is the time to enjoy a social activity that doesn't require clothing with buttons.

The most important thing about having sleepovers as an adult is reminding ourselves that we can create true intimacy with more than just the people we sleep with (or live with, or marry). We can stay up talking into the night; we can see each other with bedhead in our jammies the next morning, we can get excited over simple, childlike joys we'd long forgotten. I never feel closer to my girlfriends than when I'm chatting with them over coffee the morning after a fabulous night together. I love getting to host them as I would an out-of-town guest, to remind them (and myself) that they are just as special, and that our proximity doesn't mean they aren't worth putting in effort for.

As I get older, I have started to relish these moments even more. Most of my friends have children now, and even from the sidelines, I can see that this often means—especially for the mother—a constant prioritizing of others, sometimes at the expense of oneself. Getting the chance to make someone feel both seen and cared for, especially from someone who doesn't "have to" show them that kind of love, feels like an honor. You can love your friends actively, and, in my view, having them overnight is one of the best ways to do it.

Chapter Eight

JUST
DROPPING
BY

WHAT A "REAL ADULT" ACTS like is different for everyone and varies widely from generation to generation. While growing up, I always judged grown-ups on one key characteristic: what they did when no one was watching. It's easy to pull things together under the glare of an authority figure—as I often did, scrambling to finish my homework in the five minutes before class started—but it takes real, intrinsic maturity to *exist* in a state of Doing What You're Supposed To.

I always had a sense as a child that the grown-ups in the room knew something I didn't, prepared for outcomes I hadn't, and possessed a state of readiness that never required *getting* ready. And while my parents were always excellent at hosting their dedicated gatherings, I have distinct memories of visiting certain friends whose homes exuded that feeling of effortless preparation 24/7. In those friends' homes, there were fresh linens, a pantry stocked with brand-name snacks, solutions to any problems that arose unexpectedly, and a general feeling of safety that can only come from things being taken care of ahead of time.

There was never a rush to prepare for my arrival or a flurry of apologies over how messy things were. I didn't know what to call it at the time, but these adults *had their shit together*, and the seeming effortlessness of time spent at their home was the direct result of all the effort they had put in beforehand, when no one was looking. The pantry was stocked because it was stocked the Sunday prior, the floors were clean because they were regularly mopped, and an unexpected drop-in on my part never ruffled their feathers because the home was always ready for guests.

I am now the age many of those same parents were when I was a child in their homes. And I realize in my own adulthood that this perception I had, that idyllic image of grown-ups who always had it together, was a very shallow interpretation of what was happening behind the scenes. First and foremost, much of what seems effortless—especially as it pertains to domestic tasks—comes down to a question of money. Money for nannies and housekeepers, stocked pantries and full gas tanks, things easily replaced if they are broken or lost.

I've experienced adulthood at many different income levels, and the difference in outward appearance of competency is stark. Today, my home is pretty much always clean and my kitchen cabinets (Manhattan apartments are generally too small for a pantry) are always stocked. I keep things on hand for when I might need them in the future, and I buy things in bulk (bearing in mind space limitations) so I don't run out. I even have a short list of close friends whose dietary considerations I stay stocked for (this friend takes oat milk in her coffee, that friend is gluten-free).

It's a lovely way to live, of course, and it does make me *feel* like an adult in the way I used to view adults from the outside, but it was not always this way. For much of my twenties, when I was clawing my way out of credit card debt and barely earning enough to pay my rent, when I had a full-time job and an active array of side hustles, the kind of home I wanted to live in and the way I wanted to keep it felt completely out of reach.

Even though I was raised in a rather clean and organized home—despite our lack of resources for a cleaning service—I often let my own space fall into a state of chaos, so much so that the thought of a person dropping by on a moment's notice was incredibly scary. I felt embarrassed at how frequently I forgot to do things, how often I would default into bad spending habits because I hadn't thought ahead. (It turns out that many tiny trips to the grocery store are much more expensive than one big, thoughtful one.) This is not to say that one cannot achieve togetherness while earning a relatively low income, but that it's quite a lot harder to do so. And frequent comparisons of ourselves to people outside our tax bracket do us no favors.

Money was only half the story; the other component was what actually motivated me. Even at my most broke, I loved to see

people and to invite them over, and I felt the sting of embarrassment every time I scrambled to clean before their arrival.

Without realizing it, my early adult life—a time defined by my extreme, diagnosed anxiety—became a story of two selves: the one I could manage to scrape together when going out and the one who really existed at home. I felt like an impostor because the things that seemed so effortless for others were a complete struggle for me. And I was only making good decisions when I absolutely had to, whether enforced by a credit card company or a professional deadline. That state of being ready, of doing the work when no one was looking, felt impossible to me, and a lot of that impossibility was because of my financial reality. Without extra money to spend, and with so much time spent working for little money (first at terribly underpaid jobs, then when starting my own company), I couldn't afford to delegate or offload much of anything. It felt like I was always drowning, and only the threat of another person seeing my space was enough to snap me into action. This was the other mistake I made in assessing those adults as being so inherently *together:* It might have been second nature to them by the time I met them, but it likely took quite a lot of practice to get there.

For me, hosting became the week-to-week tentpoles of my adult-ness. Knowing that I had people who would see my apartment forced me to clean it. Preparing dinner for others meant stocking my refrigerator beyond what I needed to eat that evening. Even if I wasn't caring enough for myself to pay attention to details, I cared enough about what other people thought to become that person, at least once a week. With each passing month of living this way, the process became more and more natural to me. I began to look forward to people coming over because it inevitably buoyed my mental health.

While my anxiety was certainly an issue, I think I was too hard on myself in my interpretation of what it meant to be a grown-up. If it didn't feel effortless, I felt that there was something wrong with me. I didn't like that I needed someone watching in order to do things right, but that's a lot of what adulthood is. We create responsibilities, and then we rise to meet them; over a long enough period, we begin to meet them without really having to try.

Now I am generally prepared regardless of my social calendar and frequently have people over for drop-in visits with only an hour's notice. There is no magic to getting to this place, there is only force of habit and routine: first created for the benefit of others, then adopted naturally for myself.

There's a distinct sitcom energy to the way I live now, with a rotating cast of characters coming over unexpectedly, and me always ready with a pitcher of iced tea to pull from the fridge and some cookies to place on a serving plate. And I realize, looking back, that while some of it would have been out of reach financially, there are many aspects of how I live now that I could have implemented before on a much lower income.

I now believe there's a kind of self-fulfilling prophecy of feeling like an adult: You start to exist in a more calm, self-assured way that makes people perceive you as more mature, and thus adds to your own self-perception. But I spent many years spinning my wheels of anxiety around what other people thought, denying myself joy while also reinforcing an external image of myself as insecure and awkward. I could have felt like an adult well before I did, and I could have enjoyed my time rather than fearing someone would out me as a fraud.

This fear of having to curate a specific experience that is different from how you live prevents a lot of people from hosting. I hear from people every day who want to have more people over, who want to curate their social lives more intentionally without wasting money at overpriced bars and restaurants, but who feel intimidated to get started. Often, part of that is the delta between the way your house usually is and the way it needs to look when someone arrives.

I firmly believe that one of the most important, almost philosophical aspects of being a true hostess is this state of readiness. It's sort of like what Dita Von Teese has famously said about lingerie: You have to be wearing it for yourself, and your partner just happens to be there to enjoy it. If you wear it for them, it will always look awkward and out of place.

Frantically changing your space in order to receive guests has the same effect: Not only is it often very stressful on you, it also emits a general level of fakery that keeps you feeling anxious. Your home should be beautiful because that's the way you love to live. Your kitchen should be stocked (if you can afford it) because you take the time to thoughtfully plan your *own* food shopping. You should clean on a regular basis because you enjoy a clean, organized space (there is an entire chapter just on cleaning later in this book).

This transition was hard for me, but I have boiled it down to a few key rules, all of which I wish I had implemented sooner. The particulars of how you like your space to look and what you keep in it are totally up to you, but here are some of my best guidelines for having a home that is always ready for a friend just dropping by:

ALWAYS-READY RULES FOR YOUR HOME

1. **A FEW SIMPLE THINGS MAKE A PERFECT MOMENT FOR TWO.** While I am definitely not "dinner party–ready" at all times, I always keep a few key items in my kitchen for when people drop by. My go-tos are something fizzy to drink (I like nonalcoholic sparkling cider and Cava), a jar of olives or artichoke hearts, some roasted salted nuts, kettle chips, a block of hard cheese I can cut into shards, tea and coffee supplies, and a jar of cookies. With just those things alone, I can have an afternoon tea or an aperitif ready at a moment's notice.

2. **YOUR HOME NEEDS ITS OWN CALENDAR.** I am an avid user of Google Calendar for basically everything in my life, but I keep one for my home, too. I use it for scheduling cleaning, grocery shopping, meal planning, and other more substantial home tasks. This will allow you to stay ahead of needs before they arise.

3. **IF YOU CAN, SCHEDULE CERTAIN BULK ITEMS TO ARRIVE AT REGULAR INTERVALS.** If there are things you're always going to need—and, as is the case in places such as New York, they're hard to carry home

by hand—order them to arrive roughly when you need them. That way, you're never scrambling without, say, paper towels when guests come over (or when you need them). At my house, everything from soap to dog food to batteries are on a scheduled delivery.

4. **CUTE BASKETS ARE ALWAYS WORTH INVESTING IN.** They can hold throw blankets, toys, pet supplies, or laundry you're too lazy to fold and put away: Cute baskets are a host's best friend. Sometimes you don't have time to properly clean before a visit, or even before you go to bed at night, so having a few strategically placed baskets you can toss things into makes all the difference.

5. **IF YOU'RE GOING TO HAVE OVERNIGHT GUESTS, HAVE A GUEST BASKET.** Simple things such as hand lotion, makeup remover, tampons, tissues, and whatever else you'd want yourself on a night away from home should always be stocked in the closet for when overnight guests arrive.

6. **COOK MORE FOOD THAN YOU NEED.** I am all about pre-portioned and frozen meals, and I always cook extra when I make something. This is a great way to make sure your kitchen always feels "ready," but it's also handy when you have an unexpected guest over for a meal: There's always something homemade you can take out of the freezer and serve.

7. **A GOOD SCENT GOES A LONG WAY.** I'm still working my way up to having a signature scent for my home—I'd love to eventually make my own candles—but I do think that having a wonderful, seasonal smell when people enter your home—yourself included—makes a big difference. I usually buy candles at discount stores, like T.J. Maxx or Marshalls, but anywhere you prefer is fine.

8. **EVERYTHING ISN'T GOING TO BE PERFECT.** The more you try to micromanage every aspect of someone's experience in your home, the more impossible it will feel. There are going to be some things that aren't ready or optimal, and that's okay: You don't need to be apologizing for it.

9. **PEOPLE DON'T NOTICE THE THINGS YOU NOTICE.** On that note, it's important to remember that the little details you find glaring—the dying plant, the chipped paint, the dusty baseboards—are likely to go completely unnoticed, unless you point them out.

It may seem stressful to think of your home as a place that should always be ready to welcome people, but once you get used to it, it's actually the opposite: You realize that you don't always have to perform some elaborate routine in order to be acceptable for others. You get to share a more natural, casual version of yourself, and people get to be in your life without it being some big plan.

Some things were better in the '70s, and I would argue that the effortless socializing we see in sitcoms from that time was one of those things. People dropping by at a moment's notice was sometimes played for laughs, but it was generally seen as a happy fact of life. Doors stayed unlocked and fridges were opened by anyone who was hungry, and it wasn't expected that everything had to be absolutely perfect just to have a guest over. Caring for your home in a way that's proactive is for those who might visit it, sure, but you reap all the benefits because you get to live in a pleasant, thoughtfully curated home.

The thing about these rules, and about being intentional in the way you keep your home, is that once you start implementing them even a little bit, they become second nature. You will start to feel more confident in every aspect of your home life and more like an adult, especially when no one is looking.

"My mood sets the baseline for my guests. If I'm stressed out, so is my home. If I am distracted, so is my home. The only thing that helps (for me!) is reasonable preparation, planned rest, and only inviting people whom I enjoy. Everything else can go to shit, but if you're present and jovial, a good time can still be had by all."

—ASHLEY FORD, AUTHOR

Chapter Nine

THE
LOST
ART OF
BEING
A GOOD
GUEST

WE'VE TALKED A LOT ABOUT what it means to be a good host: the preparation, the attention to detail, the small ways to make people feel welcome (and unusually attractive) in your home. But unless you want to get stuck doing one hundred percent of the entertaining—and footing the bills that come with it—you'll want to receive an invite now and then, not just give them out. And to ensure your social calendar is full of gatherings to attend, you'll need to be a good guest.

You'll also need to curate a network of friends who enjoy taking turns playing host—it's too easy to end up in a social group where no one can even be bothered to splurge on a bag of Fritos Scoops for a movie night—but we'll save the art of creating communities for the next chapter. For now, let's focus on showing up as the best version of ourselves, something that fewer and fewer of us have been taught to do.

As we've discussed in previous chapters, the once-dominant etiquette rules have fallen by the wayside, and schools have largely gotten rid of home economics classes (which, in my opinion, should have been reimagined with a gender-neutral course rather than sidelined entirely, as domestic skills are an important part of adulthood regardless of gender). This lack of social education can result, among other things, in guest behavior ranging from mildly embarrassing to downright rude. While this is completely understandable in an economy where a growing number of people can barely afford to reliably stock their own pantries—let alone entertain friends—it also means that when we *are* invited places, we're often left without a solid set of guidelines to follow.

Making matters worse, those of us in the United States don't even have the cheat code of monocultural norms to tell us what it means to be a good guest. In two neighborhoods of the same city—or even two apartments in the same building—you're apt to encounter two entirely different minefields of faux pas. Removing your shoes might be considered the height of bizarre behavior in certain households, while it is essentially mandatory in others. Similarly, the significance of cleaning one's plate or asking for seconds can vary enormously from culture to culture. Having to navigate conflicting norms can feel overwhelming and even unfair: *"Why should I need a checklist to go to someone's house?"*

The answer is simple: Because having people over is no small thing and likely represents a lot of time, energy, and money on the part of the host. Being the kind of guest who only enhances and never burdens is simply holding up your end of the bargain. Besides, I can assure you that with a little practice, good guest behavior will start to feel completely natural and self-evident. (It essentially amounts to not being an asshole. But there is sometimes a little more to it than that.)

So, let's start with some real-life examples of what *not* to do. When it comes to piss-poor guest behavior, I've seen it all: people showing up hours late, leaving with the unopened bottle of wine they presumably brought to thank the host, or bringing an unexpected plus-one to a formal dinner. Once, I even had a guest show up with their own meal, overtaking my small Manhattan kitchen to prepare it *while I was cooking* (my eye still twitches over that one from time to time). I want to specify that being a bad guest has nothing to do with class or financial means. In fact, some of the most egregious behavior I've witnessed has come from the wealthiest people I know. I'll never forgive the acquaintance of my husband who is worth millions yet showed up at an event with a tiny dead plant I suspect he found on the street as a "gift."

I think most of us hear these anecdotes and wince even from afar, knowing instinctively that this isn't how we should behave in someone's home. But it's not enough to avoid the most extreme pitfalls: We should also start to develop a personal shorthand for how to be additive in any environment—the thoughtful type of guest who gets invited back again and again.

THE GOOD GUEST MATRIX

What it means to be a good guest will vary based on a few different factors: among them, the type of event you are attending and your proximity to the host. You can imagine a matrix—in fact, here's one opposite—that can help you determine your behavior. It takes minimal preparation to head to lunch at your best friend's place, but an intimate cocktail party hosted by your new boss? You'll want to make sure you're the kind of guest who leaves her saying, *"We should really invite them over more often!"*

So, what are the key things you need to consider after receiving an invitation? While there will always be exceptional situations and individual host idiosyncrasies, the practice of being a good guest (in my humble opinion) falls into four major categories:

HOW CLOSE IS THE HOST

CLOSE
TO THE
HOST

movie night
with your best
friend

black tie
wedding

NOT FANCY

VERY FANCY

HOW FANCY IS THE EVENT

inviting a
neighbor over
for snacks

work dinner

NOT
CLOSE
TO THE
HOST

communication, timing, gifts, and niceties. All of these are equally important and, as you'll see, have almost nothing to do with money. I repeat: *You do not need to be rich to be a good guest.* At their core, these considerations are about thinking ahead and showing basic appreciation and respect for your host. Let's get into them.

Communication

Being a good guest starts well before you arrive at someone's home. Although a seasoned host will prompt the right communication—sharing the logistics of the event, asking for any dietary considerations, telling you about the shoe policy, and so on—there are no guarantees. In lieu of these details, a good guest will proactively ask questions and offer the info their host needs to create a wonderful evening. If you have allergies or other food needs, let your host know. If you're going to be a bit late, say that. If you'd like to bring a friend or a date, ask politely—and make it clear you're open to any answer. Make sure to flag anything of note to your host well before the main event, while they still have time to make accommodations and adjustments.

One question to whip out the moment you RSVP yes: *"What can I bring?"* (And, if you have time beforehand, a *"Can I pick anything up on the way?"* is always appreciated. You would be shocked by how often a last-minute bag of ice can save the day.)

When it comes to my party contribution, I prefer to cut straight to the chase of *what*, rather than *if* I can bring something, as I've found that many hosts will tell you nothing is necessary if given the option. When you frame the question as, *"I'm going to bring something, just tell me what would be best for you,"* it relieves the host of the pressure to be polite and allows them to be honest about what would be most helpful. Sometimes they will still say nothing is necessary—in which case you can choose from a vast array of all-purpose hostess gifts (more on that later).

When *my* guests offer, I will sometimes ask them to bring a dessert or appetizer, a specific kind of wine that will pair well with the meal, or a drink mixer I'm always running out of. Sometimes I'll let them know I'm all set, in which case I am still showered with hostess gifts that I generally use at future parties. Either way, my guests are communicating clearly so that everyone knows what to expect and is primed to have a fabulous time.

Timing

When it comes to being a good guest, timing can make or break everything. In fact, if you take away only one thing from this chapter, let it be this: *Never, ever* show up to a house party early. The last twenty minutes before an event begins are impossibly stressful; having guests arrive unexpectedly while you are still very much in panic mode is a guaranteed cortisol spike for us hosts, the likes of which we rarely experience in our social lives. I personally recommend shooting for ten-ish minutes after the agreed-upon start time

to give a small grace period to the host, but that's a matter of preference. Either way, do *not* show up early.

That said, I also highly discourage showing up extremely late—especially for a more formal or seated meal. Putting on a successful multi-course meal is like producing a stage play; if you walk in during the middle of act two, you're almost guaranteed to miss something important. Showing up extremely late (in my opinion, anything over a half an hour, unless it's a very casual gathering) shows a level of disregard for the hosts and their intentions for the evening.

Lastly, it's important to never overstay your welcome. This can sometimes be difficult to judge, but I recommend looking for some of the following cues: Your host has stopped serving or offering new food or drinks, they have stopped consuming things themselves, or they have begun cleaning up and putting things away. Basically, you never want to be lingering when your host has long since wished to go to sleep, or to put them in the awkward position of having to ask you to leave. Better thirty minutes too early than five minutes too late.

Gifts

Coming well-prepared to a gathering is one of the most important habits to master as a guest. Most of us have heard by now to never show up empty-handed, but we don't often know what that means in practice. As I mentioned earlier, asking your host *what* you can bring is a great start, because often they will give you real, practical guidance. But barring that, there are two basic rules about what to bring: It should be something you know your host would enjoy and something that won't make their life harder in the meantime. For example, if your host doesn't drink alcohol (or if you're not sure that they do), don't bring a bottle of scotch. Similarly, don't bring an unexpected dish that needs to be heated in the oven or a bouquet of flowers that need cutting and arranging in a vase. Try not to create work for your host or give them an item that will need to be rehomed.

Instead, here are some evergreen ideas for hostess gifts that I default to whenever I am not asked to bring something specific:

- A bottle of something they might enjoy, like a nice wine, a high-quality olive oil or vinegar, a lovely condiment, or an unexpected mixer (I love fancy foreign sodas for this).

- An artisanal candle, either scented if you know that's something they'd enjoy or a simple beeswax pillar to throw some gentle light.

- A small item for future hosting, like fancy napkins, coasters, salt and pepper shakers, dish towels, napkin rings, cocktail stirrers, or straws.

- A food item that does not need to be served with the meal (on that note, *never* bring a surprise dish and expect it to be served—don't throw off the host's menu). I like boxes of chocolates, breakfast pastries, or fancy bar snacks.

Niceties

Lastly, each home will have its own norms and idiosyncrasies, many of them cultural. Learning to follow the general flow of an evening as your hosts demonstrate is a cultivated skill (and I still sometimes get it wrong, especially when dining with people from a culture I'm not familiar with). The important thing is to be a thoughtful observer. For example, ask if you should remove your shoes is a big consideration, because people fall on opposite sides of this particular debate. If your hosts leave it up to you but are shoeless themselves, remove your own. Try not to outpace your hosts in serving yourself, both in food and in drink, and wait for them to dictate how courses are served.

Even simple things, like not speaking at a much higher volume than your hosts, can make a huge difference. You want to be considerate of the rules of their home without having to be asked (for example, they might live in an apartment and share a wall with a sleeping baby). And similarly, making yourself a polite participant in the logistics of the evening, such as asking if you can help clear the table or serve dishes, is always a nice gesture. Especially depending on culture, you may find that your hosts insist you do absolutely nothing, but I still find that it's nice to make yourself available.

Each home you enter will be different, and as the saying goes, your presence is the present. You don't *have* to do anything to be "deserving" of community and connection—but these small, budget-friendly details make a world of difference for the people inviting you in.

We have largely lost the cultural habits around being gracious guests and take for granted what it means to have people over. (It's not just the time and expense—it's also the essential vulnerability of opening one's space and cooking skills to a group of potential critics.) Taking the time to be a good guest means saying thank you with every action, because your actions communicate clearly that you appreciate everything the host has done for you.

On that note, I want to address another lost art: that of the thank-you note. It is my opinion that a truly great guest always sends a thank-you, be it a physical note arriving whimsically in your host's mailbox several days later (my favorite) or a simple text message that expresses how lovely the evening was and highlights something that you enjoyed. It may seem like nothing at all, but remembering to thank someone—not just in the moment of leaving, but a while later, after it is no longer socially imposed—is a real act of platonic affection. We often forget that simple words of affirmation can make people feel special and seen—and can make the intricate work of hosting an event feel worth it. Giving sincere thanks on a consistent basis will make you the kind of person people want to have over again and again, because they know the effort is never wasted.

This book is primarily about hosting, yes, but I do believe that every great host is also a great guest, because they understand that both roles are fundamentally those of creating and strengthening human connection. Love is shown in many ways, and as a guest, doing things such as ensuring you are on time, bearing gifts, and paying thoughtful attention to your host's preferences is an underrated demonstration of love.

Personally, I *want* to be invited places. I want to step across the threshold and have someone take my coat while soft music and warm lighting beckon me further into the space. I want to have friends who remember to include me and are happy to see that I've RSVP'd. And for that, I need to be a great guest. It takes a little practice, but I assure you, it's worth it.

Chapter Ten

CREATING
GROWN-UP
COMMUNITIES

IT'S NOT AN EXAGGERATION TO say, much like Britney Spears, that our loneliness is killing us. One of my favorite (and I use that term loosely) stats on the subject is that loneliness is roughly as bad for people's health as smoking fifteen cigarettes per day.* Gen Z and millennials are reporting record-low levels of socialization for their age groups. We are more drained, more disconnected, more cut off from our communities and in-person networks than we've ever been, and America already had a fairly geographically isolating culture. We live physically far away from each other, we overwhelmingly rely on cars to take us places and, therefore, we rarely have opportunities to passively interact. Wages that don't keep up with the cost of living increasingly force us to work long hours, leaving little time for getting together.

As we age, Americans—especially men—find themselves with fewer and fewer friends, and it is hurting us in every conceivable way. Millennials and gen Z are, by some metrics, the loneliest generations for their respective ages, so despite the considerable negative impacts of being isolated, the problem only seems to be getting worse.

While I am always game for blaming problems on capitalism— which I very much also do in this situation—I don't like framing issues in a way that removes our own agency. Yes, we live in a social context that is built to separate us and make us increasingly reliant

---

* "3 Things Making Gen Z the Loneliest Generation," by Ryan Jenkins, Psychology Today, August 16, 2022, https://www.psychologytoday.com/us/blog/the-case-connection/202208/3-things-making-gen-z-the-loneliest-generation?msockid=30ac2a914 95e685a2adb3f22483c69e7.

on for-profit replacements for what used to be a social fabric. But that does not mean we have no tools to fight back or to make those relationships the foundation of our lives again. That reality of capitalism doesn't mean we should rule out other culprits, like the explosion of screen time among the same younger generations who are so isolated. And in my view, it isn't just a nice thing to build and maintain stronger social connections; it also gives us a major escape hatch out of the consumption-obsessed culture that's partially responsible for getting us here. The more profound relationships we have, the more loved and fulfilled we feel, and the less we need to mindlessly buy.

It is also true, however, that we need to treat building and keeping these relationships as a proactive task, because everything around us is trying to tear them down. There are also going to be contexts that make this harder. If you live far from other people, it will take more organization and time to meet with them. If you are on a strict budget, some easy options for socializing aren't going to be possible. If you're phone call–averse—as many young people tend to be—you're going to have to work harder to get the mental and emotional benefits that having long conversations provides. (Fun fact, one of the best ways to maximize the benefits of a conversation is to do it while walking: The two combined have a profound impact on our mental and physical health.*) Put simply, bonds are formed by going out of our way to form them, and in many cases that has become harder than ever.

This is more of a vibes-based argument than an empirical one, but I also think that part of our problem is a result of an overly aggressive solution to a previously flawed view of what community should be. Many of us were raised in environments where hurtful or even abusive behavior was meant to be tolerated from the people closest to you—often, your own family—and setting boundaries was considered a transgression in itself. We saw the effects that this forced proximity had on older generations, who normalized and even glorified toxic relationships because the alternative was simply not an option.

For all the economic ways we may be worse off than boomers, we at least have a more established ability to set boundaries and say

---

* "Better Together: The Many Benefits of Walking with Friends," by Heidi Godman, Harvard Health Letter, June 1, 2023, https://www.health.harvard.edu/staying-healthy/better-together-the-many-benefits-of-walking-with-friends.

no to relationships that aren't serving us. (Hell, women gained the ability to live in a financially independent way fairly recently.) But I fear sometimes that we have overcorrected, prioritizing boundary-setting and self-focused forms of care to the detriment of our relationships and communities. It's totally appropriate to cut harmful people out of your life and not feel bad about it, but the reality of maintaining important connections over the years is that it *does* sometimes require a bit of self-sacrifice. When I look at the stats on loneliness, and I hear how therapeutic language is often manipulated in service of behavior that reinforces that isolation, I worry we've gone too far in the opposite direction.

I mentioned this in an earlier chapter, but it's worth repeating: Platonic, non-familial relationships are some of the most important ones we have *because* they don't have such a high level of social reinforcement. If I am focusing this book primarily on friendship, it's because we already have extremely well-defined models for what socializing with our partners looks like (date nights), and we already typically reserve our big hosting moments for family (holidays). Profound friendships, especially as our adult lives pull us in different directions, require not just a higher level of care than many of us are accustomed to, but also the task of creating our own rituals and touchstones in the absence of the ones we've already reserved for our other relationships.

It's also a learned skill in that as far as friendships are concerned, most of us come from a model of group-based connections, with proximity as the primary connector. We make friend groups in schools and in the hobbies, sports, or activities we defined ourselves by in our early years. (Yes, this is my time to shamefully raise my hand and admit that I was a theater kid.) Our friends are often part of a larger group, so they are *also* the people we don't have to go out of our way to see.

As an adult, unless you're making most of your friends at work—and that has its own, very real set of downsides—there's not usually going to be a proximity-based friend group that simply manifests itself. I know some adults who mostly have the same core friend group from high school, but that typically requires that everyone still lives in the same geographical area (and again, I would argue that has its own drawbacks). I've seen enough *Real Housewives* to know that, occasionally, powerful adult cliques can form in certain rarified cul-de-sacs. But for most of us, even if we retain some friends from our youth, forming new relationships as an adult is going to require working muscles many of us have never had to work.

We have to make plans, and follow up, have those awkward first outings that can feel like a date without the promise of romantic infatuation. We must navigate the acquaintance phase and see which connections are worth pursuing. We even have to facilitate connections between people who don't know each other, because there isn't one gigantic group chat that drives the social calendar.

Getting out of the proximity-based friend group mentality and into one based on individual compatibility is difficult at first, but the rewards are great. For as much as we idolize the big dedicated friend group, it can be hard in practice to create true intimacy among its members. Not only are large clusters of people prone to infighting and awkward dynamics (Who gets custody of couples that divorce in the group?), they can also have a homogenizing effect, requiring everyone to assimilate in order to be accepted.

Humans naturally want to comply, and to do this within a larger group of people means assimilating into their norms and standards. By contrast, when you have various friendships or mini-groups in different areas of your life, you get to explore different aspects of yourself, serve your various needs, and not be subject to the whims and pressures of the larger assembly. To take it back to the *Real Housewives*, it always strikes me just how consumed these grown women can be by their social standing in the group. I used to experience that acutely as a teenager, but I have a hard time relating to it as an adult.

In fact, I was so anxious as a teen and twenty-something about my social performance that it took me many years (and a meaningful amount of therapy) to come to a healthier place about which relationships were actually worth maintaining. This is a little embarrassing to admit, but I used to value only the *number* of people I had in my life, even to the detriment of my own mental health, as it meant keeping "friendships" that were comically unequal or even downright hurtful. Perhaps I was correcting from the overcorrection, but I spent years running myself ragged in friend groups I didn't even like that much, showing up to events I didn't really want to attend just because I would have terrible FOMO if I didn't.

I know that especially for people like my former self, it's easy to slip back into wanting the "one big friend group," because it feels safe and affirming to be within a defined social structure. If you look at our most popular sitcoms, we affirm this model constantly. But at thirty-five, I feel comfortable and confident without the insulation of a larger group that has accepted me and, in fact, I feel mildly anxious at the thought of having to be part of one.

I've also learned that setting healthy boundaries around some relationships—the ones that are harmful or simply not enjoyable enough to pursue beyond acquaintanceship—doesn't mean there is something wrong with me, because the goal is not putting the highest score on the board.

However, we should use the energy we reclaim from saying no to the people who aren't necessarily serving us to expend it on the people who actually are. The answer can't just be to turn away from platonic connection, or to think that just because the *Friends*-style model doesn't work for us that we shouldn't try at all. For me, striking the balance between eschewing connection to an unhealthy degree and "burdening myself with unhealthy relationships," is not always easy, but there are a few questions I ask myself that help guide my path:

• **DO I FEEL LONELY?** This is a completely subjective question, but I think it's the right place to start. There have been times in my life when I felt painfully lonely, and sometimes it was when I was surrounded by the most people. Loneliness to me is the absence of true, meaningful connections—my shorthand is the people I say "I love you" with—and that has nothing to do with how busy my social calendar is. If you are feeling isolated or misunderstood, that is something to seriously consider.

• **DO I HAVE TIME FOR THE PEOPLE I LOVE?** Beyond my husband and family, I have a short list of close friends I always want to make space in my life for, even if we're separated geographically or logistically. I like to think proactively about how I can integrate them into my plans, and if I don't have time for them, I take that as a sign to look at my schedule and see where I can restore the balance.

• **HAVE I WORKED OUT A SYSTEM OF HEALTHY COMMUNICATION?** Often, adult friendships fade away because everyone is busy and everyone has a different way of communicating. Some people (like me) love long phone conversations on a regular basis while walking or cleaning the apartment; others prefer an active group chat; still others might be the type to be quiet over text but very present IRL. As silly as it might seem, communication *about* communication is the way to ensure everyone is staying in touch the way they want to, while not getting offended.

• **AM I SHOWING UP FOR PEOPLE (WITHIN MY BUDGET)?** You may not be able to join the $2,000 bachelorette trip to Tulum, but are you remembering people's big moments? Are you responding when they reach out? Are you finding ways to spend quality time together that work for both of you? I always like to ask myself what I'm giving to a relationship, before I check in on what I'm receiving.

- **ARE PEOPLE SHOWING UP FOR ME?** If you have mastered the arts of healthy communication, making time for everyone, and prioritizing your platonic relationships, you still run the risk of doing so in a very uneven way. You may find yourself in friendships that have continued on for years with only you making an effort or initiating conversation. If you are starting to feel this way about a relationship, *check in!* Go back and read your messages, pay attention to how you feel after you spend time with that person, and if it is indeed way off-balance, consider that you may need to de-prioritize this relationship to make room for others that are more reciprocal. Give people a chance and a heads-up, of course, but don't feel like you need to keep going down a one-way street forever.

- **ARE MY RELATIONSHIPS MAKING MY LIFE RICHER?** Does my life feel different when I'm showing high levels of care toward my social connections? Sometimes we frame these relationships as drains on our limited resources, but I think it's healthier to think about the ways in which our social fabric adds to our lives, so that we're encouraged to invest in it (and ourselves). It's like eating healthy: It might take a little effort in the beginning, but after a while it becomes second nature, and you'll be shocked at how much better you feel.

In many ways, adulthood has a tendency to pull us apart and define us by our differences. Choosing not to have children, for example, initially felt like a condemnation to loneliness, as nearly everyone around me made the opposite choice. I assumed that I would be excluded or forgotten, and I found myself in a therapist's chair on more than one occasion to discuss that possible outcome. And while some of my friendships have waned since children arrived, I've found that's far from the norm. In fact, motherhood has strengthened several of my closest female relationships, and I've been delighted to make friends with new women in my community who were already mothers when I met them. Yes, it requires a somewhat more thoughtful level of effort on both of our parts, but we enrich one another's lives in unique and unexpected ways when we are both willing to try.

Going out of your way to create these connections is a learned skill and is definitely less intuitive for some. Depending on where you live, there may be a natural geographic limitation to just how casually you can integrate many relationships into your life. (Some people live really far away from other people!)

But this mentality—the prioritizing of your social self, separate from work or immediate family—is worth embracing, no matter who you are. We can all be more like little Italian nonnas who gather in the town square at dusk, playing checkers and watching the children nearby. Because life is always better when people are in it.

Chapter Eleven

CURATION VERSUS CONSUMERISM

MOST OF THE WOMEN I'M truly inspired by in life could be described as *curators*, meaning they collect and create with intention. They curate their spaces and their style, they curate wonderful experiences, they curate social groups and facilitate introductions. They have discerning eyes that can see the beauty in the unexpected and know how to pull things together that are greater than the sum of their parts.

Perhaps the most typical example of this type of curator, for me, is Diana Vreeland—and if you haven't seen the documentary on her life, *The Eye Has to Travel*, I highly recommend it—but there have been many women like this, including women in my own life. Diana was a writer, a fashion editor, a visionary behind one of the most iconic magazine eras, and generally a woman whose entire life became a living, breathing work of art. Nothing about her was standard—even her appearance was unusual, especially in a world of high fashion—and her success came from her eye as a curator, a true arbiter of taste. She could look at something and see the beauty in it when few others could, and immersing herself daily in great art was key to maintaining her expertise.

Part of the reason I'm such a fan of journaling and making mood boards is because I believe that this is where curation really happens. I prefer to do this on real paper, in sketchbooks, mostly because being away from a screen helps my creativity. Much of my own taste is well outside my budget—as I think is often the case—and I use these mediums to distill everything that catches my eye into ideas I can eventually execute. In these kinds of spaces, we can see patterns and combine unexpected ideas, and in the liminal space of anticipation, there is no limit to the risks we can take.

In its best iteration, social media can help with this: With a few taps of our fingers, worlds are instantly visible to us that would have otherwise taken days, if not weeks of research. Recipes, archival photos, even intimate looks into celebrities' home decor is all there for us to collect, and ideally, to curate.

As of this writing, I've recently finished some serious renovations to my apartment. In addition to the installation of a built-in library/bar nook in an otherwise poorly used corner of my dining room, I overhauled my living room by swapping out several pieces of furniture, getting a slipcover for an armchair, and building out a wraparound gallery wall from pieces of art I've collected over the years. I'm happy to say that I stuck to my original goal of only shopping secondhand whenever possible, and I am particularly proud of the gorgeous brass-and-glass coffee table with swan-shaped legs that I scored for eighty-five dollars on Facebook Marketplace. Overall, I could not be happier with how everything came out, but I would be lying if I said that anytime I take on a project like this, there isn't a mild cost to my mental health.

Aside from the chaos of any home renovation—no matter how great your DIY skills or hired contractors are—there is also the inadequacy hamster wheel that social media can put us on when we're in curation mode. When I'm in a renovation phase, I can justify spending hours scrolling and flipping through magazines and diving into the deep end of home decor porn. Not only

am I still figuring out exactly what I want, I look at this as a time to relax my strict internet-use rules and can easily start obsessing over things that I know aren't good for me. This process can often curdle into serious envy and insecurity. For one of my newsletters, I recently wrote the following about this feeling:

> "Even if you are not prone to lifestyle inflation, certain social media behaviors will all but ensure you fall victim to it. Yes, I was able to afford things such as home renovations finally, but that just opened up a new world of content to consume, to be envious of, to feel inadequate next to. And while many of us have internalized a kind of shorthand for designer clothes or accessories—we see a Chanel bag, we know it's thousands of dollars—the world of home design is much more mysterious, even to those relatively in the know. You could have snagged a mid-century sideboard on the street for free and fixed it up, or you could have bought it on Chairish for $8,000. You could have moved into an apartment that happened to have gorgeous moldings and mantles, or you could have had them all custom-built for the price of a down payment on a home.
>
> Making things worse, the algorithmic flattening of content ensures that we never quite know what we're looking at. There are no price tags, no sense of scale, often there isn't even proper disclosure if what

we're seeing was paid for by a brand. Everyone is playing on a vastly different field, and yet we see them all jumbled together, united under the vague umbrella of "inspiration." I'm constantly recommended home decor influencers to follow, and when I go to their pages, it's a nightmare of FTC violations and deceptive labeling. That couch over there? It was gifted last year by Room & Board, but they only ever disclosed that the first time they posted it. They love highlighting that all their furniture is secondhand, but never mention that they're paying five times the average new price for things on 1stDibs. Do you like that soap caddy? You can find an amazing dupe on their Amazon Storefront!"

I want to be clear here that this kind of insecurity and social media brain rot can be found in basically any genre of consumption. We can all get lost in the influencer hall of mirrors about clothes, or beauty, or travel, or literally anything that can be monetized. (I'd guess that it's probably *more* dangerous when it has to do with your appearance. At least lusting after someone else's bathroom renovation doesn't involve reconstructing your face.) The point is, these platforms are explicitly designed to keep us on this endless loop of consumption, and the ubiquity of makeover culture only heightens it.

I had to unfollow basically any creator whose full-time job was their own home, because pretty quickly, they all fall victim to the same issue: If your home keeps looking the same way, people aren't going to stay interested. So there are overhauls for basically every season, every holiday, and every time it seems like a space has looked one way for too long.

Even hosting, which should theoretically be about the intimacy of the experience and the uniqueness of the person's home, can fall victim to the cycle of overhauling. I've also had to mute many "dinner party" accounts recommended to me, as they are a constant spiral of the most ornate table settings, lucrative brand partnerships, and elaborate dishes. It seems like these influencers never use the same materials twice (and that's likely, if it's a major part of their income). The level of effort and execution rival weddings I've attended, and even though I objectively love and enjoy my own parties, I can't help but feel that they're a bit disappointing in contrast with that perfection. It's just not good for my brain to consume this hyper-curated faux "authenticity" designed to gaslight us into thinking we're seeing a real slice of life, that what we're looking at *wasn't* paid for by a giant brand.

All of that said, I still fundamentally believe in curation and believe that the internet can be a wonderful place to do it. While I'm certainly not perfect at sticking to my own rules, even as someone who has used social media for work her entire adult life, I have come up with some basic guidelines to use when I'm seeking inspiration online. So this is my shorthand for how I navigate the internet when I'm in a time of curation, when I'm unusually vulnerable to this kind of insanity:

- **DO NOT FOLLOW PEOPLE WHOSE LIFE IS THEIR FULL-TIME JOB.** You can look occasionally, sure, but between constantly needing to renovate to keep content fresh, being filled with gifted and sponsored products, and trying to pass off the very obviously professional as the personal, these kinds of pages are simply bad for our brains.

- **DO NOT FOCUS ON SEASONALITY OR HOLIDAY THEMES WHEN IT COMES TO BUYING THINGS FOR YOUR HOME.** You do not need to redo your space every time it gets warmer, or every time a new, largely made-up holiday starts to fill store shelves around you. You do not need a themed set of dinner plates or serving tongs for every party. Most of that stuff is nonsense that ends up in storage or a landfill, anyway.

- **DO FOLLOW PROFESSIONALS (DESIGNERS, CHEFS, EDITORS, AND SO ON) WHO CREATE A CLEAR LINE BETWEEN WORK AND PERSONAL.** These people show a variety of different spaces and experiences rather than constantly having to up the ante of their own life and home.

- **DO SEEK OUT FINANCIAL TRANSPARENCY.**
Disclosing when something was gifted or sponsored should
be the absolute minimum—and it is shockingly rare—but
the more someone is open about pricing, the better it is for
your mental health.

- **DO NOT LOOK TO SPACES THAT ARE
TOTALLY DIFFERENT FROM YOUR OWN FOR
INSPIRATION.** I have a tiny kitchen, for example, so
most kitchen content just bums me out because I'll never be
able to recreate it.

- **DO LIMIT WHAT APPEARS ON YOUR FEED.**
Don't be afraid to follow accounts for certain times as you
need them for a given project or mood board. We can always
switch up what we're fed.

When I keep these guidelines in mind, I find it infinitely
easier to navigate even the most ruthlessly aspirational content.
No matter how tastefully done, influencer culture, is at its most
fundamental level, a consumerist proposition. It's about turning
the appearance of curation—of inherent style, of unique taste—
into a product you can imitate and, more importantly, purchase. I
don't begrudge anyone who's making a few bucks when someone
who follows them and buys an item they viewed on their page. But
it's the intentional conflation of personal and business, the blur-
ring of what is actually the individual's taste versus what they were

most well compensated to endorse. And I do believe that, at least to some extent, consumerism comes at the expense of curation.

For a host to master their craft, for example, they need to have wisdom about their own domain. They need to know their kitchen expertly, have a go-to list of dishes they're comfortable and confident preparing, understand their guests and anticipate their needs. There is a lived-in quality to a well-thrown party, a story behind the foods served, the glasses drunk from, the people invited.

Consumerism is about placing newness and acquisition above anything else. It's not about how thoughtfully you prepared the meal, it's about how nice the serving platter you're bringing it out on is. It's not about breaking out the well-loved items for the hundredth time because they serve you well, it's about having a full catalog of decorations for every holiday and occasion. If curation is about "less but better," consumerism is "more and worse."

Among all the examples we have of this trend, perhaps none is more acute than fast fashion (an industry that has been built, in many ways, on the back of influencer marketing). We are wearing and subsequently throwing away more clothes than ever, in staggering quantities. Our entire perception of clothing—what it should look like, how long it should last, how many pieces of it we should own—has been completely rebuilt to support a model of constant acquisition. If you've worn it once, and god forbid you've shared it on social media, it's time to move onto something new and better. I'm not really a fashion girlie, but I know that if you are, social media can be a similar game of minesweeper: How do we keep our sanity in a landscape where what we were sold yesterday is no longer good enough?

Hosting, for me, has been an antidote to this mentality. When we have become used to displaying our lives to an audience of hundreds (or more) on social media and are seeing things through a filter of what it looks like in photos, gathering intimately feels revolutionary. It doesn't matter if it's perfect, or new, or lives up to some arbitrary standard of aspiration.

What counts when people gather is how they feel. What people remember is how good the food tasted or how much they laughed in a quiet side conversation in the kitchen. Whenever I think of Diana Vreeland, I think about her New York apartment, how completely unique and frankly controversial it was. Her red-on-red-on-red drawing room, the explosions of patterns and motifs, the accumulated art and trinkets from decades of curation: It wasn't meant to be pleasing to everyone. It wasn't meant to look perfect in photos, or to be neutral enough to juice the algorithm. It was *her* in every way, and to be invited in (I imagine) was to meet her in every room you entered.

Consumerism may sometimes *feel* like curation. When we buy, we give ourselves the impression that we've come that much closer to expressing our personal style and living the life we imagine in our heads. But true artistry comes when we realize that style can exist whether or not we can afford to perfectly execute it, and that the only scale that we need to express ourselves on is the scale that makes sense for our own lives. We don't need to follow trends that don't concern us, or play to an audience that will never be satisfied. If you're feeling like you're not enough, have a few people over who you love and make them a dish you've been wanting to share. I guarantee you will feel like you have everything you need, and that how it feels is so much more valuable than how it looks.

"Invite people to help! Half of the fun of hosting is the sense of community that you just can't replicate if you were out at a restaurant. It's always best to have most of the meal prepped, but if your guests want to help set out the charcuterie, slice some bread, or get the pasta water boiling? Let them. Half the party is the wine and chatting in the kitchen, and no one wants to come over just to be waited on."

—JUSTINE DOIRON, RECIPE CREATOR AND AUTHOR OF *JUSTINE COOKS*

Chapter Twelve

CLEANING
UP

LIKE ALL THINGS IN LIFE that are good for you, learning to love cleaning and organizing is a skill that takes a lot of practice and may override your natural instincts—but it is deeply worth it in the end. Just like it takes me, on average, several weeks of cutting back on sugar to no longer crave it constantly, it takes a similar amount of time to instill good cleaning-up habits that don't feel physically painful to execute. I generally maintain a pretty tidy house these days—in part because we are two grown adults tending to it, with no kids and only a ten-pound dog who is pretty limited in the chaos she can cause—but there are definitely times when it slips away from me. And there are certain aspects of cleaning, like unloading the goddamn dishwasher, that I will never enjoy on any level. But there are things that have become intuitive for me, where I genuinely don't feel quite right if they don't get done. (I've heard some people get this way about waking up at 5 a.m. and running long distances, but that is not something I'll ever run the risk of finding out personally.)

There is great data on the fact that maintaining a clean and organized home is excellent for our mental and even physical well-being. Ultimately, we are animals, and animals thrive in a nest that is familiar and calming to them. But we also live in a culture that is constantly pushing us to acquire more and more, even if we don't have a good place to put our stuff. Visit any boomer in any American suburb, for example, and you will almost certainly find entire rooms in their home that go unused 90 percent of the time. (I'll never not be slightly creeped out by parents who preserve their child's high school bedroom exactly as it was well into that child's adulthood. At least make it a hobby room or something.) There are living rooms and sitting rooms, formal dining rooms and the kitchen islands we actually eat at, and garages full of bins holding things we can no longer even identify.

Here in New York, closet space is at an extreme premium, and yet I personally know people with wardrobes that would battle the average Real Housewife with two walk-in closets. We put things under beds and in drawers and overstuff clothing racks until they're buckling under the weight. Buying is often the way we express ourselves in this culture, and while we might mock boomers for going through life with several unused china sets in ornate mahogany cabinets, at least the things they own are generally high-quality. We are often drowning in similar quantities of the cheapest stuff imaginable, clothes and furniture that weren't even meant to last through a single move. Hoarding things, no matter how aesthetically pleasing they are, has become a default that we must move away from.

It's no wonder that shows such as *Tidying Up with Marie Kondo* were such a phenomenon, or that trends like Swedish death cleaning have caught on. We know on some level that the way we live isn't sustainable, and our brains long for the simplicity of a space where everything serves a purpose.

There is also the problem of actually *cleaning*, a different but equally important art form to organizing and downsizing. In addition to not growing up with an inherent knowledge of how to maintain things—most of my generation does not know how to sew, repair furniture, condition leather, or other tasks of longevity—and we are often clueless as to the proper ways to clean things. I think some of this is undoubtedly because, historically, these things were squarely in the domain of "woman's work."

Women were once raised with the explicit expectation that maintaining their homes—in the absence of servants to do it for them—would be their highest form of self-expression outside of motherhood. But over the decades, women have entered the workforce, and there has been no complementary revolution to bring men back into the home as equal domestic partners. (If you want a deep dive on this subject, I highly recommend the book *Fair Play* by Eve Rodsky.) Economically and socially, we have created a situation where everyone's primary focus is their profession, and the minutiae of home life is something no one really knows anything about or has time to work on. If we're both working long hours just to scrape by and keep up with the cost of living, who is going to spend the weekends scrubbing the baseboards or deep-cleaning the bathtub with bleach?

For me, learning to truly love my home and to genuinely enjoy caring for it is important for the same reason that hosting is important: It is a statement that I am worth the effort, that I deserve nice things, and that I shouldn't need to go out and pay for the experience of being in a pleasant space.

I know many people—especially in big cities—who are constantly going out because their home doesn't feel even marginally as nice as a restaurant or bar, or even a movie theater. Aside from the fact that this lifestyle can get pretty exhausting, it's also incredibly expensive. Always needing to outsource the feeling of comfort

CHELSEA'S CLEANING TIPS

For big cleans, create a spreadsheet with columns for each room and cells for each task within that room. Tackle your cleaning room by room, graying out the cells as you go.

Consolidation is a key part of cleaning: Combine near-empty containers of things, remove clothes you no longer wear, and get rid of any "maybe I'll need them" items you haven't used in years.

Chic baskets are your friend, especially in a small space. Have a few baskets in each room where you can store things you frequently use but don't want to see lying around.

Reset the kitchen, make your bed, and sort/put away laundry every day; the rest you can get away with doing weekly.

At least twice a year, clean all the things that never get noticed, such as your upholstered furniture. Yes, that includes investing in an upholstery cleaner.

Order your go-to cleaning supplies to be delivered on a regular schedule, so that "not having what you need to clean" is never a reason not to.

Make sure every room has more of what you might need within reach as part of cleaning: toilet paper in your bathroom, soap in your kitchen, coasters in your living room.

Every time you finish a big clean, light a fresh candle to celebrate.

and luxury means paying a premium for it. Making my home a place I actively want to stay in was a huge part of my initial push to get better with money. I learned to be genuinely okay with zero-dollar days at home because I liked being there, and I discovered the things I was often seeking when I went out were things I could recreate on my own.

We talked a little in a previous chapter about how I approach decor and how I set up my home for visiting guests. These things are important, of course, and are as much about personal expression and creativity as they are about mental well-being. But I would argue that keeping a clean and organized home is equally important, even if your space is still very much a work in progress. You don't need to wait for some idealized version of your place for it to be worth taking care of. Looking back, I wish I had shown more care toward the crappy apartments I lived in in my early twenties. I definitely did not take them seriously, and I felt that because they weren't what I wanted from an aesthetic point of view, I didn't need to waste my time making them "perfect." But there was so much more I could have done to keep them nice, and I think I would have felt much more confident and at ease if I had, knowing that I treated myself and my surroundings with respect even if they weren't particularly fancy.

Today, I have a set of rituals that keeps me on track when it comes to cleaning, and I'm a big proponent of spreadsheets to make it easier. I will admit that living in a smaller space—my apartment is around eight hundred square feet—definitely has its advantages when it comes time to clean. But even in a bigger house, breaking the task down into bite-size pieces helps it to feel manageable and easy to integrate into the rest of your day. Here's how I think about it:

- **DIVIDE AND CONQUER.** If you live alone, this is all on you—and trust me, I've been there. But if you live with people, you must first and foremost decide who is in charge of what, and actually hold each other accountable to the tasks. I say this with all the love in the world to my fellow hetero sisters: If your man is not taking on equal responsibility in housekeeping, if you have to constantly remind him or micromanage him or do things for him, stop. Take a step back and understand that this is not just a red flag in terms of compatibility, but also in terms of mutual respect. This is something to be addressed at the most fundamental relationship level and not something you should spend your whole life making do with. See what happens when you stop micromanaging, make yourself heard, and, most importantly, do not just accept that this is something you have to "own" because you happen to be the woman in the relationship. Fair division of labor in the home, now!

- **BREAK IT DOWN.** I have a spreadsheet I use religiously for my cleaning. I used to use one for weekly cleaning, but now I only really need it for the quarterly deep clean, because the rest has become intuitive. But anytime it feels overwhelming, I use my sheet: I break the apartment down into rooms, and then tasks within each room. Each task gets its own cell, which I gray out as I complete it. I go room to room until every cell on the sheet is gray, and then I know I've actually done one hundred percent of the cleaning.

- **HAVE DIFFERENT ROUTINES ON DIFFERENT TIMELINES.** There are things we do every day, like make the beds, empty and fill the dishwasher, wipe down counters, and take out the trash if needed. We have our weekly duties, like cleaning the bathroom or changing the sheets. And then there are the monthly-to-quarterly tasks, like wiping down the shutters, cleaning under the beds, donating unused items, or polishing the hardwood floors. Writing down what your timelines are and what happens in each of them removes the guesswork of constantly wondering what you forgot to do until you notice it's a mess.

- **ALWAYS BE PURGING.** The only way to truly gain control over your space is to become ruthless about what gets to stay in it. We are all creatures of nostalgia, and we are all prone to keeping things we absolutely will never need or use again. For me, an entire row on my spreadsheet is dedicated to decluttering, because I need to make a point of regularly purging items, or it won't happen. If I haven't worn a clothing item in two seasons, goodbye. If we don't play a board game, we give it away. Old makeup, expired medicine, used-up candles, empty boxes? Be gone from here.

- **DO THE SIMPLE THINGS THAT FEEL FANCY.**
When you're giving your home a deep clean, it's always nice to find little ways to go the extra mile for yourself. Even something as simple as fluffing pillows, shining surfaces, folding the last sheet of toilet paper, or checking to make sure soap dispensers are full helps give you that "in a hotel from the comfort of your own home" vibe. Part of feeling happy and comfortable in your space is knowing that things are taken care of, and it's easiest to work in those little touches when you're already cleaning or organizing.

- **STOCK WHAT YOU'LL NEED.** One thing I always do is keep extras of the things I know I'll always need on hand, so I never run out. Paper towels, trash bags, dishwasher pods, laundry detergent, face wash, and cleaning spray are always kept in stock in our hall closet or storage unit—we have most of them scheduled for regular delivery—and buying them in bulk gets us a much better per-unit price. Not having to constantly run out for things and instead anticipating your own needs before they become an issue will always make your home feel like a happier place to be.

- **REWARD YOURSELF WHEN IT'S DONE.** I have little rituals I always work into my cleaning routines to make them something I look forward to. For my quarterly deep cleans, for example, I always get myself a new scented candle that I only light when everything is fully cleaned. I'll often order takeout for dinner on those days, too, as I'm usually too tired to cook and it gives me something really indulgent to enjoy in my fresh space. Even for my more regular cleaning, I'll save a good podcast or audiobook I've been wanting to listen to for when I know I'm doing a dreary activity (like laundry, something I loathe), so that it feels more enjoyable in the moment. Treating ourselves like kids who need to be incentivized with candy is perfectly fine, as long as it gets the job done.

In our current era of overconsumption, and of treating the things we already own like afterthoughts, there's something special about taking a high level of care in your space. It's not just for when other people visit—although, as we've discussed, keeping things in a presentable state is always very helpful for when guests drop by— it's about realizing that we deserve to live somewhere beautiful and clean. We deserve the nice little touches, the organized drawers and fresh-smelling sheets and sparkling tiles. I also believe that if we're really focused on enjoying what we have, we're much less likely to be drawn in to wanting more. We understand the work it takes to truly maintain things and are less inclined to bog ourselves down with more things that will need maintaining.

Real love for our homes isn't some mindless "restocking" video where a disembodied hand is putting hundreds of single-use plastic items into bigger plastic containers. It's not about having everything hyper-organized and color-coded and every cabinet bursting at the seams with more. It's about figuring out the things that are truly important to us, understanding what makes us feel most "at home," and leaning into that.

Back in my studio apartment, with barely enough money to stock the refrigerator (let alone overstock it), I thought I didn't deserve to show that kind of love to the place I lived. I thought I needed abundance in order to take pride in my home. Today, I understand that real abundance is knowing what you need, having it when you need it, and treating it well in the meantime. When done right, cleaning your home is a spiritual practice, and one that makes everything we do within it feel that much more enjoyable.

Chapter Thirteen

PLAYING
THE
LONG
GAME

WHEN I WAS AN AU PAIR in France, the grandmother of my host mother would often come by the apartment to see the children. She was already nearly a hundred years old when I met her and lived many years beyond that, long enough to see her oldest great-grandchildren start their adult lives. She remembered watching the parade of American soldiers when France was liberated in World War II, she was famous for her ratatouille, and I never saw her without her outfit perfectly styled and every hair in place.

It was the first time I'd ever known someone of that age—my own living grandmother was in her eighties at the time, something that felt a world away from three-digit numbers—and it felt impossible that someone could have spent so many years on this planet and still be so much a part of it all. It was my first year living in the country when I met her, and it left a profound impression on me: Life doesn't simply stop when we get older, and we don't have to pretend that it does.

In the years following, first living in France and then spending much of every year there with my in-laws, I realized she was not as much of an anomaly as I had initially thought. Yes, French people do live longer than Americans on average (people in most developed countries do), but it also has a culture not nearly as ageist as what we've become accustomed to. You see it in big and small ways: actors on television—even, *gasp*, women!—have visible wrinkles and gray hair. Restaurants and bars and even concerts have wide age ranges joining in the fun, and it's not at all unusual to see a much older person out on the town past midnight. Elders gather in town squares and visit markets and play chess in the park and

are generally woven into the fabric of society in a way we don't see nearly as much here in the United States.

There is real statistical truth to this—perhaps unsurprisingly, older adults are reportedly happiest in the Nordic countries*—but you also feel it on a very human level when you're there. And it's not just France, of course—that just happens to be the country I'm most experienced with outside of the States. This is true in so many places around the world, where age is considered something to respect, rather than something to hide away.

I made the choice years ago to only follow influencers above a certain age on social media—the rule is generally somewhere around fifty—because of the hugely beneficial effect it had on my mental health. Our culture is youth obsessed, yes, but our social media platforms are all the more so. If we don't actively work to fight it, we will be drowning in a sea of beauty-filtered, line-free faces, blindingly white veneers, and headlines screaming about which celebrity is aging most "unproblematically" these days. Seeing women who are older and make no effort to hide it, who have gray hair and lines at the corners of their eyes, who talk freely about the (sometimes imperfect) paths they've taken to self-acceptance feels revolutionary. I love watching them in their second and third acts, getting a window into all of the life they feel entitled and empowered to enjoy.

We speak sometimes about "taking up space" as it pertains to marginalized identities, and that is exactly what I think when I

---

* World Happiness Report 2025, https://worldhappiness.report/?embed=true.

see these vibrant older women. They are reclaiming their rightful place in society, and are not ashamed of it. It should not have felt as revolutionary to me as it did at the time that the woman I met as an au pair, even at nearly one hundred years old, still enjoyed life to such a palpable extent. Without realizing it, I had internalized the idea that women just sort of disappear at a certain age, scurrying off to some vague retirement compound or sitting in their home with knitting needles and a television permanently tuned to the home shopping network. Now, every day when I open my social media feeds, I'm awash in women of all ages going on full-fledged adventures and documenting it without apology, because they are not going to waste one moment of their precious lives on this earth afraid to actually *live*.

For me, the strong social connections we form when we are younger is a key ingredient to this recipe as we move through life. We've discussed how literally sick loneliness makes us, but even for people who manage to remain in good physical health, once we are off the playing field of social life, it can be incredibly intimidating to get back in the game. The way in which older people are simply folded into the fabric of daily life in many other cultures is a question of social connection, of feeling included without having to ask if they can participate.

When I'm walking down the street here in Manhattan and see a group of much older women pass me on a tour, I think: *that's it*. If we do not have people around us who love us at every stage of our lives, it gets harder and harder every year to put ourselves out there. I want to be the fabulous older woman who goes on trips with her friends to Italian wine country or Mexico City. I want to feel as essential to my community then as I do now, and the work to get there starts early.

Part of the reason hosting (and being hosted) is so important is that, for better or for worse, much of our "outside" socializing is currently very youth oriented. Most bars are nightmarish to be in past the age of thirty. Even restaurants seem to be constantly upping the ante on how loud they can play the music during dinner service. Outside of certain jazz bars or concert halls, much live music can be inhospitable to people who don't essentially want to be in a mosh pit, and even your average workout class can be unwelcoming to people who aren't already in an ultra-fit young body. Our culture puts up all kinds of barriers to aging while still being part of the party, and by taking our social lives back into our homes, we get to decide the terms. We can play music we like at a volume we enjoy, we can accommodate people's dietary needs, and we can do it all at a reasonable hour. For many of us, outside of the drinking culture of college and our early twenties, where the social calendar revolved around going somewhere unpleasant and then drinking enough to make it bearable, there wasn't much of a guidebook on how to gather.

I want us to create homes we love and then welcome people we love into them, because that is something we can enjoy at any age—and without having to feel like we're crashing the party. It's in these intimate moments that we can truly get to know each other, and nothing about a dinner party has to be stuffy or prudish. We can break out of the pop culture–driven notion of socializing past a certain age as inherently boring or entirely forgotten. We don't have to fall off the cliff of party culture into a wasteland of never socializing at all. There is a middle ground, and the best way to create these bonds is to start enjoying each other's company now, in a way that doesn't require being young and in a skintight mini dress, shivering outside a nightclub.

At least in my corner of the internet, there's been a recent resurgence of all things Nancy Meyers. Young people love her interior designs, the luxurious ways she styles food, the subdued palettes, and the sense that there are no real problems in her characters' lives. But I also think part of this fascination is how unashamedly she centers older people in her movies, particularly older women. *It's Complicated* has always been one of my comfort movies, and I don't think I would enjoy it nearly as much if Meryl Streep weren't exactly as old as she was, still getting to have all of that delirious fun. There is a comfort in the aesthetics and storytelling, sure, but also in knowing that an elegant and adventurous life can still await us, and that there are many excellent things that come with getting older, rather than just the oft-repeated downsides. It feels like a warm embrace from a possible future, and a vision of women having a fabulous conversation around a dinner table at twenty-plus years older than I am right now.

The thing about Nancy Meyers movies is that they've definitely mastered how to create a wonderful space and to make the characters feel wonderful in it. Their homes feel like dreams you don't want to leave, and their refrigerators are always stocked with fresh iced tea and leftover cake. Their accumulated wisdom translates to a sense of ease and belonging to the people who enter their orbit, and while it's never explicitly framed as "being a hostess" in the tradition of a Martha Stewart or even an Ina Garten, there is that same sense that these are women who *know* things, and who've already thought a few steps ahead to make sure you can relax and enjoy yourself.

In a culture that relentlessly values youth, it's refreshing to celebrate the luxuries of being a little more mature. Being a hostess is one of the few skills in life that we only develop and improve at with age, as we accumulate a more interesting and lived-in home and get more comfortable with having people in it.

Many of us were lucky enough to have much older women in our lives as children who always made us feel special and taken care of when we visited them, who made our favorite recipes or set up the guest room just right for our arrival. I remember sitting in the kitchen of my late grandmother's Florida home, the sound of the wall clock ticking as she watched me eat my peanut butter sandwich on the white bread I was never allowed at home, crusts dutifully removed. I remember the smell of her perfume and the impeccable pouf of her hair at the crown of her head, the smart little outfits she would put on her tiny frame, even just to go to the grocery store. I remember the little carved elephant figurines on the lacquered sideboard in her living room, how everything felt so glamorous and mysterious, like a little girl's idea of a five-star hotel.

To be a guest in a such a home is to experience those simultaneous joys of familiarity and newness, the warmth of being welcomed with the frisson of possible surprise. Everything is a little different than we are used to, but everything also feels accessible. And in the presence of this energy, we become a little more ourselves, a little more charming and easygoing and quick to laugh.

To be a true hostess means to love through action, to create a space for people to bloom within, to anticipate their needs before they even have to ask. It is the chance to create a connection that can last decades, because a good dinner party is always in style, and a hit recipe is something people will come back to enjoy at every stage of their lives.

We are creatures of seasonality. Unfortunately, particularly here in America, we are so focused on the early days, the springtime of things when all of the big moments are happening in rapid succession. We celebrate the graduations and the engagements and the weddings and the babies, and then there is a long pause, and an eventual fading into a time when we are rarely celebrated at all. Having people over is a way to reclaim each season of life, to firmly state that *you* decide what is worth throwing a party for, and that *you* will be the one to throw it. It is a defiant stance that life is only short if we cram all of it into the beginning and wait around for someone else to give us permission to enjoy the rest.

I submit that life is long, actually, and that there is always room for one more at our table.

Happy hosting.

ACKNOWLEDGMENTS

THERE ARE SO MANY PEOPLE to thank for this book, starting first and foremost with my family, especially my mother, who first taught me the art of hosting. Thank you to my forever agent Anthony Mattero and my longtime editor Libby Burton—*dare I say the dream team?*—for I fear we may have done it again! Thank you to the many hostesses who lent tips for this book. Thank you to my Financial Diet team, for letting me do fun stuff outside of work, and for steering the ship so marvelously in my occasional absence. Of course I must also thank my art team on this book, particularly my wonderful illustrator Layla and my photographer Chelsea, who nailed the exact tone of sophisticated whimsy we were going for. And no acknowledgments would ever be complete without thanking my darling husband Marc, the Jeffrey to my Ina, the Paul to my Julia, the one who makes everything worth doing.

ABOUT THE AUTHOR

CHELSEA FAGAN IS THE CEO and co-founder of The Financial Diet, an author, a social media creator, and a home cook. She has published four books, *I'm Only Here for the WiFi*, *The Financial Diet*, *A Perfect Vintage*, and *The High Dive*.

Ten Speed Press
An imprint of the Crown Publishing Group
A division of Penguin Random House LLC
1745 Broadway
New York, NY 10019
tenspeed.com
penguinrandomhouse.com

Typefaces: Dutch Type Library's DTL Fleischmann, Monotype's Sackers Gothic, Adobe's Leander Script

Library of Congress Cataloging-in-Publication Data is on file with the publisher.

Hardcover ISBN: 978-0-593-83686-6
Ebook ISBN: 978-0-593-83686-6

Editors: Libby Burton and Cristina Garces | Production editor: Ashley Pierce
Editorial assistant: Cierra Hinckson
Designer: Lizzie Allen | Production designers: Mari Gill and Faith Hague
Production: Jane Chinn
Photo assistants: Nicholas Beaudet and Angela Cholmondeley
Copy editor: Andrea Chesman | Proofreaders: Allie Kiekhofer and Daina Penikas
Publicist: Kristin Casemore | Marketer: Andrea Portanova

Manufactured in China
10 9 8 7 6 5 4 3 2 1

First Edition

The authorized representative in the EU for product safety and compliance is Penguin Random House Ireland, Morrison Chambers, 32 Nassau Street, Dublin D02 YH68, Ireland, https://eu-contact.penguin.ie.